First World War
and Army of Occupation
War Diary
France, Belgium and Germany

16 DIVISION
Divisional Troops
77 Brigade Royal Field Artillery
1 October 1914 - 31 December 1916

WO95/1962/3

The Naval & Military Press Ltd
www.nmarchive.com
Published in association with The National Archives

Published by

The Naval & Military Press Ltd

Unit 10 Ridgewood Industrial Park,
Uckfield, East Sussex,
TN22 5QE England
Tel: +44 (0) 1825 749494

www.naval-military-press.com

www.nmarchive.com

This diary has been reprinted in facsimile from the original. Any imperfections are inevitably reproduced and the quality may fall short of modern type and cartographic standards.

© Crown Copyright
Images reproduced by permission of The National Archives, London, England, 2015.

Contents

Document type	Place/Title	Date From	Date To
Heading	WO95/1962-3		
Heading	16th Division 77th Brigade R.F.A. 1914 Oct-1916 Dec To 1 Army		
Heading	B.G.F 17.2.16-1914 Oct-1916 Dec		
War Diary	Cahir Co: Tipp:	01/10/1914	01/10/1914
War Diary	Fermoy	20/11/1914	11/08/1915
War Diary	Rollestone Camp Salisbury Plain.	04/08/1915	04/08/1915
War Diary	Deepcut	30/08/1915	30/08/1915
War Diary	Bordon Camp.	04/12/1915	04/12/1915
War Diary	Larkhill Camp.	05/01/1916	05/01/1916
War Diary	Bordon Camp	11/01/1916	16/02/1916
War Diary	Le. Havre	17/02/1916	17/02/1916
War Diary	On. Train	18/02/1916	18/02/1916
War Diary	Berguette	19/02/1916	22/02/1916
War Diary	Isberqure	26/02/1916	08/03/1916
War Diary	Lieres.	08/03/1916	08/03/1916
War Diary	Bordon	15/02/1916	16/02/1916
War Diary	Southampton Docks	16/02/1916	16/02/1916
War Diary	Havre	17/02/1916	18/02/1916
War Diary	Lillers	19/02/1916	19/02/1916
War Diary	Ham	24/02/1916	26/02/1916
War Diary	Berguette	29/02/1916	29/02/1916
War Diary	Bordon	17/02/1916	17/02/1916
War Diary	Southampton	17/02/1916	17/02/1916
War Diary	Le Havre	19/02/1916	19/02/1916
War Diary	Sanvic	21/02/1916	21/02/1916
War Diary	Berquette	22/02/1916	22/02/1916
War Diary	St Quentin	26/02/1916	26/02/1916
War Diary	Guarbecque	08/03/1916	08/03/1916
War Diary	Ecquedecques	26/03/1916	03/04/1916
War Diary	Corons De Rutoire	05/04/1916	03/07/1916
War Diary	Berguette	03/03/1916	03/03/1916
War Diary	Lieres	08/03/1916	28/03/1916
War Diary	Berguette	01/03/1916	08/03/1916
War Diary	Lieres	08/03/1916	13/03/1916
War Diary	Fosse 7	14/03/1916	14/03/1916
War Diary	Lieres	19/03/1916	30/03/1916
War Diary	Bordon	16/02/1916	16/02/1916
War Diary	Southampton	16/02/1916	16/02/1916
War Diary	Havre	17/02/1916	18/03/1916
War Diary	Lillers	19/02/1916	19/02/1916
War Diary	Ham	19/02/1916	26/02/1916
War Diary	Berguette	26/02/1916	08/03/1916
War Diary	Lieres	08/03/1916	31/03/1916
War Diary	Lieres.	13/03/1916	29/03/1916
War Diary	Berguette	01/03/1916	08/03/1916
War Diary	Lieres	09/03/1916	08/04/1916
War Diary	Westrehem	09/04/1916	09/04/1916
War Diary	Lieres	11/04/1916	16/04/1916
War Diary	Fosse 6	19/04/1916	29/04/1916

War Diary	Lieres	01/04/1916	04/04/1916
War Diary	In The Field	05/04/1916	30/04/1916
War Diary	Lieres	03/04/1916	07/04/1916
War Diary	Westrehem	08/04/1916	08/04/1916
War Diary	Lieres	09/04/1916	09/04/1916
War Diary	Fosse 7 (Vermelles)	11/04/1916	25/04/1916
War Diary	Loos Front.	27/04/1916	31/04/1916
War Diary		14/04/1916	23/04/1916
War Diary	Lieres	01/04/1916	01/04/1916
War Diary	Vermelles	03/04/1916	10/04/1916
War Diary	Lieres	11/04/1916	14/04/1916
War Diary	Fosse 7	15/04/1916	30/04/1916
War Diary	Lieres	04/04/1916	15/04/1916
War Diary	Verquin	16/04/1916	30/04/1916
War Diary	Fosse 6	01/05/1916	30/05/1916
War Diary	Maroc	01/05/1916	31/05/1916
War Diary	Fosse 7	30/04/1916	18/05/1916
War Diary	South-Maroc	18/05/1916	30/05/1916
War Diary	South-Maroc		
War Diary	Philosophe	01/05/1916	30/05/1916
War Diary	Fosse 7	04/05/1916	30/05/1916
War Diary	Fosse 6	02/06/1916	30/06/1916
War Diary	Philosophe	01/06/1916	28/06/1916
War Diary	Maroc (M 2 B 33/2 Sheet 36 C S.W)	01/06/1916	30/06/1916
War Diary	G.33.a. 4.5.	01/06/1916	30/06/1916
Heading	War Diary 77th Brigade Royal Field Artillery 1st. July to 31st. July 1916.		
War Diary	Fosse 6	01/07/1916	31/07/1916
War Diary	Corons De Rutoire.	06/07/1916	06/07/1916
Heading	War Diary 77th Brigade RFA Month Of August, 1916. Volume. 7		
War Diary		01/08/1916	30/08/1916
Heading	War Diary 77th Brigade RFA. For Month Of September, 1916 Volume. No 8.		
War Diary	Vecquemont	01/09/1916	02/09/1916
War Diary	Ville	03/09/1916	03/09/1916
War Diary	Bray	04/09/1916	04/09/1916
War Diary	Maricourt	05/09/1916	05/09/1916
War Diary	Maurepas	06/09/1916	25/09/1916
War Diary	Maurepas & Angle Wood	25/09/1916	26/09/1916
War Diary	Combles	27/09/1916	30/09/1916
Heading	War Diary Month Of October, 1916 Volume 9 77th Brigade RFA Vol 9		
War Diary	Carnoy Talmas	01/10/1916	01/10/1916
War Diary	Amplier	02/10/1916	02/10/1916
War Diary	Vacquerie	03/10/1916	03/10/1916
War Diary	Heuchin	04/10/1916	04/10/1916
War Diary	Quiestede	05/10/1916	05/10/1916
War Diary	Godewearsvelde	06/10/1916	08/10/1916
War Diary	Westoutre	09/10/1916	31/10/1916
War Diary		07/10/1916	07/10/1916
Heading	War Diary For Month Of November, 1916. Volume 10. 77th Brigade R.F.A. Vol 10		
War Diary	Fermoy Farm N.13.d. 2.O (Near Locre)	01/11/1916	30/11/1916
Heading	War Diary For Month Of December, 1916. Volume 11 77th Brigade RFA Vol XI		

War Diary   Fermoy Farm. N.13.d. 2.O (Near Locre)   01/12/1916   31/12/1916

NDRT/1962 (3)

16TH DIVISION

77TH BRIGADE R.F.A.
~~FEB — JUN 1916~~

1914 OCT — 1916 DEC

TO 1 ARMY

77th Bde
R.F.A.
16th Div

Vol 1

B37 17.2.16.

France 16

1914 Oct — 1916 Dec.

Army Form C. 2118

WAR DIARY
or
INTELLIGENCE SUMMARY

"B" Battery. 77th Bde. R.F.A.

(Erase heading not required.)

Instructions regarding War Diaries and Intelligence Summaries are contained in F. S. Regs., Part II. and the Staff Manual respectively. Title Pages will be prepared in manuscript.

Place	Date	Hour	Summary of Events and Information	Remarks and references to Appendices
CAHIR. Co. TIPP.	1/10/14		The Battery was originally formed on this date as 242nd Battery R.F.A. from which B/77th Bty. forms for recruits in the 1st New Army & mobilized at the Depot Preston. It was then ordered to be a 6 gun battery. 2nd Lt. F. RIGBY commanded the Battery which was given 15 horses for training purposes.	
FERMOY.	20/11/14		The 77th Brigade marched to FERMOY. Colonel KENT commanding. Captain FRENCH Adjutant. Bty/G. was marched from H.Q. Depot ATHLONE. 3/12/14 – 80 men. 6/12/15 – 15 men.	
	23/1/15		The designation of the battery was changed from 242nd to B. Battery 77th Bde. The establishment returned to that of a 4 gun battery. from Tues Oct 1914 1915 the average number of horses was 25. Drill was carried out on an 12 Pr. that gun. It was was practices on Howitzers found D. Battery.	
	1/2/15		40 men transferred to the newly formed D. Battery.	
	22/5/15		The Battery was inspected by Brig. Genl. Rathbone Comdg. 16th Divl. Arty.	
	21/12/14		Major A. MEALY arrived to command the battery.	
	7/10/14		Lt. O.S. BURNE joined the battery.	
	17/8/15		" B.G. LEE " " "	
	11/8/15		" S.B. JENNER " " "	
			The Battery left FERMOY 30/8/15 entrained to DUBLIN camped 2 days in Phoenix Park. Embarked at NORTHWALL
ROLLESTONE CAMP SALISBURY PLAIN.	4/9/15		& arrived by HOLYHEAD to AMESBURY. 46 horses – entrained in Ireland. The remainder of the 16th Divl. Army was transferred to the New Army's Division. The 77th Bde: went to DEEPCUT by order Lt. Col. T.F.W. TIPP. C.R.A. was appointed of 77th Bde. BORDEN 483/15
DEEPCUT.	30/8/15		The Battery received 4 – 4.5 How's. completed establishment of horses, horses in s/qtr for gun practice on
BORDEN CAMP.	4/12/15		Travel to LARKHILL CAMP. Canadian lines for gun Practice. on 5/1/16.
LARKHILL CAMP.	5/1/16		Gun Practice from 5/1/16 till 9/1/16.

Army Form C. 2118

WAR DIARY or INTELLIGENCE SUMMARY

(Erase heading not required.)

Instructions regarding War Diaries and Intelligence Summaries are contained in F.S. Regs., Part II. and the Staff Manual respectively. Title Pages will be prepared in manuscript.

Place	Date	Hour	Summary of Events and Information	Remarks and references to Appendices
BORDON CAMP.	10/2/16.		Relieved by Guns from LARKHILL.	
	12/2/16.		Remainder of Divl. Arty. were equipped less the battery completed drawing. Horses were in good condition. Very little ordered – no rain likely.	
	14/2/16.		Drew to close bayer, reinant etc.	
	16/2/16.		Major A.E. NEWLAND took over command of the Battery.	
LE HAVRE.	17/2/16.		The Battery entrained in two lots at 5.30 a.m. & 6.30 a.m. Left Southampton at 7 p.m. on board S.S. BELLEROPHON. with cruiser also ½ B.A.C. 182 Bde. + D/182.	
			After steaming about ½ the dist. for 16 hours in a heavy sea & gale of wind, the ship got alongside at 10 a.m. & were ordered to travel to DOCKS REST CAMP until 8.0 a.m. 18/2/16.	
			One hour was utilised with "Rumouring" & few deficiencies in equipment made up.	
ON TRAIN	18/2/16.		Entrained at Point 3. left at 11.30 a.m.	
BERGUETTE.	19/2/16.		Arrived BERGUETTE. (PAS DU NORD) about 9.30 a.m. – detrained & marched to HAM (BUSSEY) & BUILES.	
	20/2/16.		Heavy rain & frost with old weather. Horse lines in a bog. No casualties of any sort on journey from England.	
	22/2/16.		Guns were waiting from Railhead.	
ISBERQUES.	26/2/16.		Marched to ISBERQUES in snow storm & hard frost. Horses drew very few hundred yards. Had been unable to obtain frost cogs were told to "make up nails". Were offered no iron. Had brought a supply of nails from England – but nails were no use on the hard frost.	
	5/3/16.		G.O.C. R.A. R.t Corps. inspected Divl. Arty.	
	8/3/16.		2/Lt. R.E. INGRAHAM joined on posting. Two Officers, 2 N.C.O.s, 6 Gunners & 6 Signallers to D/85. 12th Divn. at VERMELLES.	
			Left by Route march for LIERES. G.O.C. R.A. 16th Divn. inspected Bde. on road. Expected turning very pleased with Battery turn out.	
LIERES.	8/3/16.		Instructions issued commenced. Battery detailed for instruction D/65 – 12th Divn. + B/75–15th Divn. G.O.C. artillery during weather reformed. One Gunner slightly wounded by shell splinter in last day of course. Every morning during weather specimen were dressed & battery in France. Horse lines still in mud with little or no shelter.	

77th (How) Brigade RFA

30-3-16

Army Form C. 2118.

WAR DIARY
or
INTELLIGENCE SUMMARY.
(Erase heading not required.)

Place	Date	Hour	Summary of Events and Information	Remarks and references to Appendices
Borden BORDON	Feb 15/16	—	77th (How) Brigade R.F.A. entrained at BORDON STATION en route for SOUTHAMPTON DOCKS and HAVRE. The Brigade was conveyed to the DOCKS in 10 Trainloads. The following details of officers entrained with the Brigade:—	
			Bde H.Q. Lieut Col J.Mc-Taggart — Brigade Commander	
			" Capt C.A. Mortimer — Adjutant	
			" Lieut R.D. Briscoe — Orderly Officer	
			" Lieut R.E. Hoskins R.A.M.C. Medical Officer	
			A/77 Capt R. Steen — Battery Commander	
			Lieut R. Williamson	
			Lieut Jas Hughes	
			Lieut T.C. Hepworth	
			B/77 Major A.E. Newland D.S.O. Battery Commander	
			Lieut J.B. Tonner	
			Lieut D. Burke	
			Lieut F. Lee	
			C/77 Capt J.T. Pirie — Battery Commander	
			Lieut J. Phirt-Evans	
			Lieut C.F. Avice	
			Lieut T. Cyffty	
			D/77 Major L.A. Cotton — Battery Commander	
			Lieut J.R. Sneggie	
			Lieut H. Price	
			Lieut K.G. Kelly	

77 (How) Brigade RFA

Army Form C. 2118.

WAR DIARY
or
INTELLIGENCE SUMMARY.
(Erase heading not required.)

Place	Date	Hour	Summary of Events and Information	Remarks and references to Appendices
Bordon BORDON	Feb 15/16	—	R.A.C/77 Major J.A. Hunter Column Commander. Lieut. D. McAliobin Lieut T.H. Going R.S.M. Herron Brigade Sergeant Major	

Personnel

Battery	Offr	W.O.	Sar.	Cpls	Bdr	Gnrs	Drs	Total
Bde H.Q.	4	1	2	2		12	13	36
A	4	1	8	5	9	59	55	141
B	4	1	8	4	9	61	54	141
C	4	1	8	6	9	56	56	140
D	4	1	8	5	9	61	51	139
B.A.C.	3	1	5	4	5	27	64	109
Total	23	6	39	26	43	276	293	706

Horses

R	D	Total
27	15	42
43	87	130
43	88	131
42	87	129
41	82	123
19	118	137
215	477	692

Vehicles

Guns	Ammn Wagons	4 Wheel	2 Wheel	Cycles
—	—	5	2	1
4	8	2	2	1
4	8	2	2	1
4	8	2	2	1
4	8	2	2	1
—	16	3	1	1
16	48	16	11	6

SOUTHAMPTON DOCKS Feb 16	—	The Brigade embarked on 3 ships at SOUTHAMPTON DOCKS and after a stormy crossing landed at HAVRE on Feb 17th.
HAVRE Feb 17	—	Rest Camps. HAVRE
HAVRE Feb 18	—	Brigade entrained and proceeded up country
LILLERS Feb 19	—	Brigade detrained at LILLERS (B Battery at BERGUETTE) and marched to billets at HAM near BLESSY — distance about 10 miles
HAM Feb 24	—	Brigade drew its ammunition B (Shrapnel) from LE RÉVEILLON BX (H.E.) from TREIZENNES The following ammunition was drawn

	B	BX	Total
Battery	42	390	432
B.A.C.	74	694	768

	B	BX	Total
Brigade	242	2254	2496

77th (How) Brigade RFA

Army Form C. 2118.

3

WAR DIARY
or
INTELLIGENCE SUMMARY.

(Erase heading not required.)

Place	Date	Hour	Summary of Events and Information	Remarks and references to Appendices
HAM	Feb 28	—	Brigade moved billets from HAM near BLESSY to BERGUETTE by march route. Distance about 8 miles. Owing to a heavy fall of snow and consequent poor road was in a very slippery condition but the march was carried out without casualties to men or horses.	
BERGUETTE	Feb 29	—	The Brigade was inspected in column of route on the road near GUARBECQUE by the G.O.C. R.A. 1st Corps who discussed his opinion after appearance and turn out of men & horses	

Army Form C. 2118

B/77.R.F.A. Vol I XVI

WAR DIARY
or
INTELLIGENCE SUMMARY
(Erase heading not required.)

Instructions regarding War Diaries and Intelligence Summaries are contained in F.S. Regs., Part II. and the Staff Manual respectively. Title Pages will be prepared in manuscript.

Place	Date	Hour	Summary of Events and Information	Remarks and references to Appendices
BORDON.	17/2/16.	9.0. A.M.	Left for LIPHOOK STATION to entrain for Active Service.	
SOUTHAMPTON.	"	8.10. P.M.	Embarked.	
LE HAVRE	19/2/16.	11 A.M.	Disembarked and proceeded to No.2.Rest Camp SANVIC.	
SANVIC	21/2/16.	12 Noon.	Entrained at LE HAVRE. Snowing.	
BERGUETTE	22/2/16.	3. P.M.	Detrained and proceeded to Billets at ST.QUENTIN. AIRE. Still snowing.	
ST QUENTIN.	26th	9.0. A.M.	Proceeded by road to GUARBECQUE and went into Billets.	
			2 Officers and 15 N.C.O's and Men were attached to 12th Divisional Artillery for instruction from 1st to 4th March and a similar party from 5th to 8th of March.	
GUARBECQUE	8/3/16.	11.0. A.M.	Proceeded by road to ECQUEDECQUES and went into Billets. One section consisting of 2 Officers 2 Nos.1. 12 Gunners and 6 telephonists and 1 Cook attached to 12th Divisional artillery for instruction from 9th to 12th March.	
ECQUEDECQUES	26/11.0. 3/16. A.M.		Right Section proceeded by bus to CORONS DE RUTOIRE and were attached to C/70 Bde R.F.A. for instruction.	
	3/4/16 Noon.		Took over completely from C/70.Bde.R.F.A. REMAINDER of Right Section and the Left Section proceeded to Gun and Wagon Lines of C/70., Wagon Line being at NOEUX LES MINES.	
CORONS DE RUTOIRE	5/4/16.		General Alexander V.C. visited Gun Line. Zones registered.	
	4/3/16.		2/Lt.L.W.Heath.R.F.A. taken on strength of Brigade and posted to this Battery.	
	30/3/16.		2/Lt.D.S.F.Mackenzie.R.F.A. -do-	
	27/4/16.		No.31445.Gnr.Gillingham.J.C. wounded in action and died of wounds in Hospital same date. No.31554.Gnr.Lacey.L. wounded in action. Gas attack at 4.30.A.M.	
	28/4/16.		Battery position heavily shelled until noon. Battery shelled continuously from 9.45.A.M. to 4.30.P.M.	

WAR DIARY
or
INTELLIGENCE SUMMARY

(Erase heading not required.)

Army Form C. 2118

Place	Date	Hour	Summary of Events and Information	Remarks and references to Appendices
CORONS DE RUTOIRE.	29/4/16	5.30 am.	Gas Attack - Battery position shelled until midday - No. 31441, Gnr. Kern A.W. wounded in action and taken to hospital	
	30/4/16	6.0 am.	Battery position shelled with 5.9's and 8" - also lachrymatory shells - No.104552, Dvr. Berwick T. killed in action.	
	11/5/16	8.30 am.	Battery position shelled until 10.0 am. during which time No. 31283, Gnr. Fairminer A.F. and No.31356, Gnr. Gould L.W. were badly wounded.	
	12/5/16		2nd. Lt. D.S.F.Mackenzie R.F.A. proceeded on course of Gunnery etc. at R.A. School, MAZINGARBE. - 2nd. Lt. Anderson (T.F.) R.F.A. attached for instruction.	
	14/5/16		2nd. Lt. G.B.Anderson (T.F.) R.F.A. completed course of instruction and returned to ENGLAND to rejoin own unit.	
	21/5/16		2nd. Lt. D.S.F.Mackenzie R.F.A. completed course and rejoined unit.	
	23/5/16		2nd. Lt. F. Pusey R.F.A. transferred to Brigade Headquarters and appointed Orderly Officer. 2nd. Lt. J.A.Murdock, R.F.A. transferred from Brigade Headquarters to this unit.	
	29/5/16 9/6/16		2nd. Lt. F. Carpenter, R.F.A. taken on strength of Brigade and posted to this unit. 2nd. Lt. W.H.F.Ollis,R.F.A. wounded in action and admitted to Hospital.	
	2/6/16		Change of designation - "D"/177 Brigade R.F.A. transferred to "A"/77 Brigade, R.F.A. and now known as "A" Battery, 77 Brigade, R.F.A.	
	8/6/16		Battery position shelled continuously throughout the day, about 300 shells in all.	
	10/6/16.		Right Section of "A"/178 Brigade R.F.A. (40th.Division) attached for instruction.	
	23/6/16 2/7/16 3/7/16 3/7/16		2nd. Lt. L.W.Heath, R.F.A. and No. 32956 Sgt. Grain H. proceeded on leave. 2nd. Lt. L.W.Heath,R.F.A. and No. 32956 Sgt. Grain H. returned from leave. Attached Section left to take up its position in the line at BULLY GRENAY. 2nd.Lt.L.W.Heath, R.F.A. proceeded on course of Gunnery etc. at R.A. School, MAZINGARBE.	

WAR DIARY of 77 (H) Bde Arm Bde Army Form C. 2118
RFC
INTELLIGENCE SUMMARY
For March 1916

(Erase heading not required.)

Place	Date	Hour	Summary of Events and Information	Remarks and references to Appendices
BERGUETTE	5/3/16		Arrival of 2/Lt Davis to replace 2/Lt S. M. McAlister who had been previously posted to D/77	
LIERES	9/3/16		The B.A.C. moved to LIERES along with the Brigade	
	9/3/16		2 Officers (2/Lt T.H. Going & 2/Lt H.H. Davis) and 6 N.C.O's proceeded to 65/73 A & 10th Division at VERQUINEUL for instructional purposes. Duration of the Course 30 days.	
	13/3/16		Major Heather O.C. B.A.C. Sergt Major Harper, Sergt Dryhurst, Cpl Donson likewise proceeded to 65th Bde Am Column until the 16th. Officers & N.C.O's were struck by the case with which ammunition could be rapidly sent to the Batteries by the formation of a B.A.C. forward dump.	
	21/3/16		The B.A.C. was inspected by the G.O.C.R.A. 16th Div. Gen. Duffus C.B. who expressed great satisfaction with the general turn-out.	
	26/3/16		2/Lt T.H. Going and Gunner Henderson (70421) left for a course of instruction at the Trench Mortar School, with the view to permanent posting in that unit.	
	29/3/16		The 77th How. Brigade was inspected by the Corps Commander, General Monro & was complimented on its fine appearance	

T.F. Davies
2/Lt for OC 77 Howitzer
BAC

Army Form C. 2118.

WAR DIARY
or
INTELLIGENCE SUMMARY.

77th (How) Brigade R.F.A.

(Erase heading not required.)

Instructions regarding War Diaries and Intelligence Summaries are contained in F. S. Regs., Part II. and the Staff Manual respectively. Title pages will be prepared in manuscript.

Place	Date	Hour	Summary of Events and Information	Remarks and references to Appendices
BERGUETTE	1/3/16		1st Phase of training of 16th Div. Art. commenced with the despatch of a certain number of officers, NCOs & gunners. Signallers &c to the front for training with batteries of 1st, 12th & 15th Divisions	
"	6/3/16 8/3/16		2nd Lts ROBERTON, INGRAHAM, HAMILTON joined and were posted to A/77, B/77, C/77 respectively. The Brigade moved billets from BERGUETTE to LIERES by march route, and were inspected on the march by the G.O.C. R.A. who expressed his approval at the appearance and turn out of the men & horses	
LIERES	8/3/16		Instructional training at the front continued - another party of officers, N.C.Os & men from Batteries of this Brigade proceeded to the front for attachment to batteries of 1st, 12th, & 15th Divisions	
FOSSE 7 LIERES	13/3/16 14/3/16 19/3/16		1st Battle Casualties:- S.S. HAMMOND A/77 & Gunr HATTON B/77 received injuries as result of shell explosions at the front. Section training at the front commenced 2/Lt W/3.C. or acting Captain, and 1 subaltern, 2 NO 1, 4 Signallers & 1-12 gunners from each Battery went up to the Gun line, & 4 NCOs & drivers & 28 drivers from each Battery & Wagon lines of Batteries of the 3 above mentioned Divisions - attached for 1 week. The Brigade Commander & 4 Signallers of 77th Bde H.Q. went to the front to be attached to 3rd Bde H.Q. & 73rd (How) Brigade R.F.A. - 15th Division	
"	26/3/16		2nd party of Sections as above started for the front for training	
"	27/3/16		Report from G.O.C. 15th Div Art. through G.O.C. 16th Div. Art expressing his gratification on the latter upon the receipt from the former of an excellent report upon the general of batteries of 77th Brigade attached for instruction to units at the front	

77th (How) Brigade R.F.A.

Army Form C. 2118.

WAR DIARY
or
INTELLIGENCE SUMMARY.

2

Place	Date	Hour	Summary of Events and Information	Remarks and references to Appendices
LIERES	28/3/16	4pm	Inspection of Brigade by G.O.C. 1st Army at ECQUEDECQUES - (Sir CHARLES MONRO) G.O.C. 1st Army expressed his satisfaction with the appearance & turn out of the Bde	
"	29/3/16		C Battery, which has previously drawn for the lot of Counter-battery, left the Brigade and marched to NOEUX-les-MINES - for attachment to the Heavy Artillery of the 1st Corps. C Battery had previously handed over 3 howitzers to 30th Battery whose howitzers were being repaired - To complete C Battery to its full equipment on its departure to join the Heavy Artillery, 3 howitzers of D/77 were therefore sent to C/77	

Army Form C. 2118.

A.A.A RFA

WAR DIARY
or
INTELLIGENCE SUMMARY.

(Erase heading not required.)

Instructions regarding War Diaries and Intelligence
Summaries are contained in F. S. Regs., Part II.
and the Staff Manual respectively. Title pages
will be prepared in manuscript.

Place	Date	Hour	Summary of Events and Information	Remarks and references to Appendices
BORDON	16.2.16	10 am	Left section entrained at BORDON STN for SOUTHAMPTON	
		11 am	Right " " " "	
SOUTHAMPTON	"	2 pm	Arrived SOUTHAMPTON	
	"	5 pm	Embarked	
	"	8.30 pm	Left SOUTHAMPTON	
HAVRE	17.2.16	9 am	Arrived, disentrained and marched to rest Camp (HAVRE) remained the night in tents	
"	18.2.16	7 am	Marched to GARE DES MARCHANDISES	
			Entrained	
LILLERS	19.2.16	8 am	Arrived LILLERS, detrained and marched to HAM near BLESSY.	
		10 am	Troops Billeted in barns. Horses in the open	
HAM	19.2.16	10 am	Remained in HAM	
	20.2.16		" "	
			Nothing of importance to note	
	26.2.16		Marched to BERGUETTE	
BERGUETTE	26.2.16	10 am	Arrived. Troops billeted in barns and Houses. Horses in the open	
	26.2.16	4 pm	"	
	27.2.16		Nil	
	28.2.16		"	
	29.2.16		One NCO went on course of Anti Aircraft observation; attached to 22nd A.A.Bty, at SAILLY LABOURSE	
	1.3.16	10 am	Nil	
	2.3.16		2 Drivers joined the Battery to replace 2 sick evacuated	
	3.3.16			

Army Form C. 2118.

A/77 RFA

WAR DIARY
or
INTELLIGENCE SUMMARY.

(Erase heading not required.)

Instructions regarding War Diaries and Intelligence Summaries are contained in F. S. Regs., Part II. and the Staff Manual respectively. Title pages will be prepared in manuscript.

Place	Date	Hour	Summary of Events and Information	Remarks and references to Appendices
BERGUETTE	4.3.16		nil	
	5.3.16	9am	CAPT SPENCER & 2Lt HUGHES with 12 signallers proceeded to Bergueth position near NOVELLES to be attached.	A/65
	6.3.16		nil	
	7.3.16		nil	
	8.3.16	10.50am	Battery inspected to LIERES	
LIERES	8.3.16	1pm	Arrived. Troops billeted in Barns. Right Section horses under cover of sheds and barn. Left Section in the open. Up till the present none of the battery horses signs of falling away from the bad weather and a hoven distemper affecting the clipped ones.	
	9.3.16		nil	
	10.3.16			
	11.3.16		Party sent up to the front on 5.3.16 returned, also NCO from SAILLY LABOURSE	
	12.3.16			
	13.3.16			
	14.3.16		nil	
	15.3.16			
	16.3.16			
	17.3.16			
	18.3.16			

A/177 RFA

Army Form C. 2118.

WAR DIARY
or
INTELLIGENCE SUMMARY.
(Erase heading not required.)

Instructions regarding War Diaries and Intelligence Summaries are contained in F.S. Regs., Part II. and the Staff Manual respectively. Title pages will be prepared in manuscript.

Place	Date	Hour	Summary of Events and Information	Remarks and references to Appendices
LIEBES	19.3.16	7.30am	CAPT SPENCER, Lt HUGHES 5# NCOs & 17 gunners & drivers sent up to be attached to C/73 Bty at MAROC. Rcvn then took over a section of guns. Drivers installed in wagon lines duties.	α 28 horses
	20.3.16 to 25.3.16		NIL	
	26.3.16	2.30pm	Party sent to C/73 on 19th returned	
			Lt ALLHAUSEN and similar party (but without horse) proceeded to C/65 Bty near NOYELLES	
			1 NCO sent to course at the Anti Gas School	
			4 NCOs and 12 men a draft from A/65 to replace drivers sent to A/65 from this battery.	
	27.3.16		NIL	
	28.3.16	4pm	The Brigade was inspected by G.O.C. 1st Army near ECQUEDECQUES.	
	29.3.16 30.3.16 31.3.16		NIL	

[signatures]
Claude A/177

Army Form C. 2118

WAR DIARY
or
INTELLIGENCE SUMMARY
(Erase heading not required.)

Instructions regarding War Diaries and Intelligence Summaries are contained in F. S. Regs., Part II. and the Staff Manual respectively. Title Pages will be prepared in manuscript.

Place	Date	Hour	Summary of Events and Information	Remarks and references to Appendices
LIBRES.	13/3/16		2nd Lieutenant party went to B/85 - 12th Divn:	
	19/3/16		B.C. 1 officer, 2 N.C.O. & 12 gunners went to Gun Position of B/73 – 15th Divn: at Fosse 7 de May Loos. for 1 weeks instruction. 4 N.C.O., 12 Gunners & 28 horses went to wagon line relieve battery.	
	22/3/16		G.O.C. R.A. 16th Divn: inspected horse lines & gun P.n.P.	
	25/3/16		Above party returned.	
	26/3/16		2nd Section for instruction went to B/85 came through as above except that N.C.O. & gunners went to wagon line B/85 without horses & the same number of N.C.O. & gunners from B/85 came by tramp for duty with the battery.	
	27/3/16		Report from G.O.C. 15th Divl. Arty. that G.O.C. 16th Divn. Arty approving certain gratification will exempt report on personnel of battery attached to battery of 15th Div. Arty for instruction.	
	28/3/16		Inspection of B.C. at 11.0pm by G.O.C. 2nd Army. at Esquerdecques.	
	29/3/16		G.O.C. 2nd Army expressed his satisfaction with our appearance of Bde. further expressed views. Since arrival of B.attery, horses out of stable were exercised went buying weather. There were few horses which had been clipped all over – The majority only their legs. to keep was will up to date there have been no case of strept. catters (received) to show trouble of linked hide. he horses were cast. 2 through injuries (accidents), 2 though other injuries & 2 Remount cases as unsuitable to type. Very little sickness amongst men. bit external – eczema, one litter – epistaxis & one farmer slightly gassed but unwounded. The average sick parade numbers 2. All minor injuries & colds.	

M. E. Lindsell
Major R.F.A.
Cmdg. B/177 Bde. R.F.A.

Army Form C. 2118

WAR DIARY
or
INTELLIGENCE SUMMARY

D/77th Bde R.F.A.

(Erase heading not required.)

Place	Date	Hour	Summary of Events and Information	Remarks and references to Appendices
BERGUETTE	1st March 1916		Major E.B. Potter & 2/Lt. Rice J. & 138 O.R.s of Right Section were attached to 10/65th Brigade R.F.A. at Hory for three days. 2/Lt. W.M. McAlister joined 10/77th Bde. R.F.A. from 77th Brigade A. Col.	
	2nd		B.S.M. Richards, B.Q.M.Sgt. Miles, Sergt. Ames were admitted into Hospital at BUSNES suffering from Influenza.	
	4th		Brig. General Duffus inspected horse lines of 10/77th Bde. R.F.A.	
	5th		Major E.B. Potter, 2/Lt. Rice J. & Right Section returned from Hory. B.S.M. Richards, B.Q.M.Sgt. Miles, Sergt. Ames discharged from Hospital at BUSNES	
	8th		Left BERGUETTE for LIÈRES	
LIÈRES	9th		2/Lt. K.G. Williams & 2/Lt. W.M. McAlister went with part of Left Section to Hory & were attached to 110th Battery.	

WAR DIARY
or
INTELLIGENCE SUMMARY

Army Form C. 2118

Place	Date	Hour	Summary of Events and Information	Remarks and references to Appendices
LIERES	12th March 1916		2/53. R.G. Williams, 2/53. N.M. McAlister, also part of Reg. Y. returned to LIERES.	
	13th		Major E.B. Potter, 2/58, Lieut R.G. Williams & part of Left Section were attached to "10"/3rd. Bde. R.F.A. for three days. 2/53. Price E. with part of Right Section were attached to "10th Battery for three days.	
	14th		Gunner Hatton J. slightly wounded in head, shoulder while attached to "10"/3rd Bde. R.F.A. by fall of earth owing to bursting of a High E. shell.	
	16th		Personel of N.M. a Bde. R.F.A. attached to Batteries as above returned. Gr. Hatton J. admitted into Hospital at LILLERS.	
	17th		Brigade Route March.	
	18th			
	19th		2/53. R.G. Williams, 2/53. N.M. McAlister along with part of Left Section left for Front & were attached to "10"/65th 13 Bde. R.F.A.	

WAR DIARY
or
INTELLIGENCE SUMMARY

(Erase heading not required.)

Army Form C. 2118

Place	Date	Hour	Summary of Events and Information	Remarks and references to Appendices
LIERES	20th March 1916		Gunner Hatton J. returned to Duty.	
	26th		2/Lt K.G. Williams & 2/Lt D.M. McAlester also part of Regt X returned from Front. Major E.B. Potter, 2/Lt T. Pierce with part of Regt 9 Section proceeded to Front 9 men attached to 10/3rd Bde R.F.A.	
	29th		G.O.C. 158 Army inspected 77th Brigade R.F.A. 10/77th Bde. R.F.A. handed over three guns to (H) to 75 Bde R.F.A.	
	30th		B.S.M. Scroggie C.R. joined 10/77th Bde from Hospital. 2/Lt M.C. Bears attached to 10/77th Bde. R.F.A. for duty	
	31st		I.O. 77th Brigade R.F.A. inspected the horse lines of 10/77th Brigade R.F.A.	

77th (How) Brigade R.F.A. — 77 RFA Vol 3

WAR DIARY
or
INTELLIGENCE SUMMARY

Army Form C. 2118.

XVI

Place	Date	Hour	Summary of Events and Information	Remarks and references to Appendices
LIERES	3/4/16		2 Storylus orders issued for Battery in Lieu of Horses — Left and Right Sections of B/77 fired on the front on 30 in in rotation, relieving certain B Cy/3 — Similarly B/77 three Right Section of Major General T. Morene to the lower lines of the Batteries, who expressed	
"	8/4/16	3 p.m.	his satisfaction with the appearance and condition of the horses	
WESTRECHEN	9/4/16		Remainder the Brigade at LIERES, consisting of B & A HQ. B/77 and RHQ/77 took part in a route march and tactical exercise in conjunction with 15th Divisional Training	
LIERES	11/4/16		From LIERES with B/77 returned to LIERES from the Front — Major Newland and right section of B/77 relieved a section of B/73 at FOSSE 7	
"	12/4/16		The relief of B/73 by B/77 was complete	
"	13/4/16		One section of B/77 relieved a section of B/73 at FOSSE 7	
"	15/4/16		Relief of B/73 by B/77 was completed	
"	16/4/16		Brigade Head Quarters moved from LIERES to FOSSE 6 relieving the Brigade H.Q. of 73rd (How) Brigade R.F.A.	
FOSSE 6	19/4/16		The Batteries continued firing daily in retaliation for the enemy's shelling and in registration of the various targets taken over from the 73rd Brigade Lieut N.A. Lane posted to D/77	
"	22/4/16		Inspection of Brigade Ammn Col. Lines at VERQUIN by Brigade Commander	
"	23/4/16		Inspection of A, B and D sub-sections by Brigade Commander	
"	24/4/16			
"	27/4/16		Between gunners launched an attack on our front lines & gave in conjunction with an intense bombardment of our front aid support trenches in its POSTS 14 BIS and HULLOCH Sections. After about half an hour the enemy lifted his artillery fire on to communication trenches & gun positions. B.6 Battalion at FOSSE 7	

WAR DIARY or INTELLIGENCE SUMMARY

Army Form C. 2118.

77th (How.) Brigade R.F.A.

Place	Date	Hour	Summary of Events and Information	Remarks and references to Appendices
			were heavily bombarded with lachrymatory and high explosive shells — at about 5.30 am under cover of the fire German Infantry parties entered our front line trenches near the CHALK PIT. About B/77 the officers of the LONE HOWITZER at the CHALK PIT observed two Germans entering the CHALK PIT at the Northern end, as the infantry had already evacuated the trench, and it was impossible to remain with the gun owing to the dense cloud of gas which settled in the pit. Lieut the Hon. E/ decided to abandon the gun. The lights of the gas however, but probably owing to keep the front facts to ignite the charge. Gunner Medicott B/77 was shot through the head and killed whilst attempting to leave the CHALK PIT. The behaviour of all ranks was excellent under this trying and experience of a real action. This situation communication was maintained with the enemy from a few minutes by the Divisions who regularly if trying to retaliate, but on opening the said the Line Lieut. Legg in the Cross of the Brigade HQ Staff was killed which remains to brigade were near FRAIE 7, and his name was forwarded in the issue of ... FR. Q.M. 2A for special notice in connection with the work of the Brigade.	
			Owing to the heavy expenditure of ammunition it was found necessary to replenish ammunition of Brigade L.F. Batteries was put a stress on the personnel to be wagon lines etc. be allowed to accompany the wagons being up ammunition.	
FRAIE 6	29/4/16		A second gas attack was made from the direction of PUITS 14 BIS and HULLUCH at 3.50 am. The officers artillery for (9 the 16th Bri Art) carried out the fire gas officer, on a point of 200 yards. The enemy to support his ground the Front, was driven back to the trenches by some sound of the gas officer.	

A Battery 77th Brigade R.F.A.

Army Form C. 2118.

WAR DIARY
or
INTELLIGENCE SUMMARY.
(Erase heading not required.)

Instructions regarding War Diaries and Intelligence Summaries are contained in F. S. Regs., Part II. and the Staff Manual respectively. Title pages will be prepared in manuscript.

Place	Date	Hour	Summary of Events and Information	Remarks and references to Appendices
Lucheux Gorres	1.4.16	—	Nil	
	2.4.16		Nil	
	3.4.16	1 p.m	Left Section left for Moeux-les-Mines arriving about 4 p.m. Taking over wagon lines and gun pits from C/73rd Bde R.F.A.	
	4.4.16	1 p.m	Right Section left for Moeux-les-Mines arriving about 4 p.m. 15th Divl Artillery.	
In the Field	5.4.16		Nil	
	6.4.16		Nil	
	7.4.16		Nil	
	8.4.16		Nil	
	9.4.16		Nil	
	10.4.16		Nil	
	11.4.16		Nil	
	12.4.16		Nil	
	13.4.16		Nil	
	14.4.16		Nil	
	15.4.16		Nil	
	16.4.16		Nil	
	17.4.16		Nil	
	18.4.16		Nil	
	19.4.16		Nil	
	20.4.16		Nil	
	21.4.16		Nil	
	22.4.16		Nil	
	23.4.16		Nil	
	24.4.16		Nil	
	25.4.16		Nil	

D.H. Hopwell Lt.
for O. Cawdly Capt.
A/77 Bde. R.F.A

Army Form C. 2118.

WAR DIARY
or
INTELLIGENCE SUMMARY.
(Erase heading not required.)

Instructions regarding War Diaries and Intelligence Summaries are contained in F. S. Regs., Part II. and the Staff Manual respectively. Title pages will be prepared in manuscript.

Place	Date	Hour	Summary of Events and Information	Remarks and references to Appendices
Left of line	26.4.16			
	27.4.16	6.30am	Fired 8.3 Rds at Night Lines (Enemy Gas Attack.)	✗
		8.30am	Fired 89 Rds at Night Lines (Enemy Gas Attack)	
		3.10pm	Fired 8 Rds at Enemy on Parapet	
		7.0pm	Fired 28 Rds at Night Lines (Enemy Gas Attack)	✗
		7.30pm	Fired 23 Rds at Pent 44 bis (Orders from Brigade)	
	28/4/16	8.25am	Fired 8.44 Rds at hostile Support Line Hill 40 (In retaliation)	✗
		6.30pm	Fired 2 Rds at Estaminet working Party	
		9.15pm	Fired 28 Rds at Night Lines (Gas Alarm)	
	29/4/16	11.15am	Fired 42 Rounds at Night Lines (Enemy Gas Attack.)	✗
		9.15am	" 16 " " Orders from	
		9.30am	" 3 " " Brigade	
		5.30pm	" 16 " at Suspected Gas Plant	
		6.30pm	" 1 " at Mm seen inflicting damage of previous 16 rayed	

L.H.Ripwell 2/Lt
for O. Connog 2/77 "B" Bde. 16 FA.

2353 Wt. W2544/1454 700,000 5/15 D. D. & L. ADSS./Forms/C. 2118.

Army Form C. 2118.

WAR DIARY
or
INTELLIGENCE SUMMARY.
(Erase heading not required.)

Instructions regarding War Diaries and Intelligence Summaries are contained in F. S. Regs., Part II. and the Staff Manual respectively. Title pages will be prepared in manuscript.

Place	Date	Hour	Summary of Events and Information	Remarks and references to Appendices
In the Field	30/4/16	—	Nil	

Shipwell R.S.A.

fr O Ewing A/77 +3d. R. F.A

Army Form C. 2118

WAR DIARY
or
INTELLIGENCE SUMMARY
(Erase heading not required.)

Instructions regarding War Diaries and Intelligence Summaries are contained in F.S. Regs., Part II. and the Staff Manual respectively. Title Pages will be prepared in manuscript.

73 Battery 77th Brigade R.F.A.

Place	Date	Hour	Summary of Events and Information	Remarks and references to Appendices
LIERES.	3/4		Establishment of Resting Notes retired from 4.2 to 40 Kingdir issued in lieu.	
	4/4		I.D. Returns to visit brothers uniforms brought forward. This Cell remains	
	5/4		C.O.E. 16.? Diff. Arty. visited was also visited by Bde. was filled with bros, bivis roll arrangements. Major I.W. F. Mercer also visited Battery & expressed his satisfaction, afterwards staying.	
	7/4		Route March to Durieuse Training Ground in conjunction with 15 Divon on infantry Battery	
WESTREHEM.	8/4		Coop of position in a relieve of defence. Retiring to billets at WESTREHEM.	
LIERES.	9/4		Returned from Divl. Training.	
FOSSE 7. (VERMELLES)	11/4		B.C. & 2 officers went "section" (Regnt.) completed took over duties at Gun position & wagon lines of B. Battery 73rd Bde. The filled places of B/73 took over the 2 Vickers Guns of the battery	
	12/4		Two officers & the remainder of the Battery completed the relief of B/73 by 6.0 p.m. Guns were left in situ by said Battery.	
	13/4		The Battery fired for the first time in the campaign. Two Zones were laid out experiment? etc in laying arrangements. B. Littler, G. Munson & J. McEdowres posted to Trench Mortars Battery	
	14/4		Duty firing in retaliation for enemy's shelling in registration. Battery working steadily since taking my god. Great dose - improvement in armament & activity of augurs.	
	23/4		Capt. Laws moved with fire, showing finds to certified visual observation. Carried on and sir O.P. in front. 2.4.: B.H. Laws RFA posted to Battery	
	25/4		At 10.30 a.m. O.P. was set alight by sea cartridge fire of M.E. Mercer. Four typewriters & binoculars	

WAR DIARY or INTELLIGENCE SUMMARY

Army Form C. 2118

Place	Date	Hour	Summary of Events and Information	Remarks and references to Appendices
LOOS FRONT	29/4		We were on duty at the time Claude [Lowther?] arrived of final approval in notifying were withdrawn almost immediately. The Bde. Commander sent his congratulations on this conduct to the wire party.	
		At 5 am	The Germans attacked the 14 Bde. & Hulluch Sectors of the 11th Divisions Front with two Divisions. Wells & Gas [discharges] accompanied by an intense bombardment of front trenches. Thunder of 30 min. bombardment then lifted onto [Barrage?] of communication trenches, Artillery positions & points in rear. Batteries ceased out the one section's position entirely and knocked out [several] guns, but by 11.30 am our guns were quieting and the one section. The rest of the day was quiet. The enemy poured fire on supply lines from the front. Main [line?] from Bt. was turned below Bates. The enemy shelling of town & our interchange all along to A.O.P. There were upward communication without [discontinuity?] on the "gas attack" also 410 rounds were fired. Up to 11.30 am. A quiet day. Germans were suspected of intention to repeat this gas attack.	
	29/4	At 10 am	the Germans again attacked with gas on the Ypres front. In this sector the wind changed & blew the gas back over them. They were forced to evacuate their front line trenches for a length of 1000 y. to attack was made. A.O.1 [Pumpful?] was about [numbers & guns?] Thanks. Page up the use of gas & changed from the Ypres but the Bn. Supper was the connection with the enemy's days [?] ceased. The enemy was quickly trounced by the Bde. Commdr. Lt. Captain [Freyalum?], Lt Buckle, Lieuts Miller, [Henry?] [Lance?] Corpns. Pte. Murray, Pte. Perkins, Pte. Thomas E., Pte. Taylor. During the two days operation this was great competition amongst all ranks in the scoops these to accompany the [Wagon?] taking up ammo. Men had to be brought up in any [way?] were very upset [indeed] to	[remarks column – partially legible notes about the occasion, the gas being used by the Enemy, the Battery Gunners men who took up guns to the first line, and other notes]

WAR DIARY
or
INTELLIGENCE SUMMARY

(Erase heading not required.)

Army Form C. 2118

Place	Date	Hour	Summary of Events and Information	Remarks and references to Appendices
LOOS FRONT.	29/4		Weather still fine.	
	3/5		Quiet day. Wind wrong for the use of gas.	
			At 9.30pm an SOS very light sent up from Pt Alain front. A battalion of the left Brigade was attacked, successfully but officially reported the attack.	
			The D.C.C. 16th Div. Arty ordered through the Res Comm. his Brains with the officers was to get before some arrangements at the Weapon Line in charge of 6 Trenches during the assault — 3. Chyfty trench requires orders.	
			" " — 2. minor injuries.	
			" " — 6.10am	
	14/5 23/5		For this week on the 27th & 28th April, the 16th Dist. Arty. received the thanks of the Infantry Brigadiers concerned & the G.O.C. 16th Divn.	
			To HQ. the attached account specialisation in Trench Mortars.	

A. N. ....
Major R.A.
Comdg. B/77 R/A

Army Form C. 2118.

B Battery 77th Brigade RFA

Page I

WAR DIARY
or
INTELLIGENCE SUMMARY

(Erase heading not required.)

Place	Date	Hour	Summary of Events and Information	Remarks and references to Appendices
Lieres	April 3		Major E.B. COTTER, Lieut. PRICE's right section went up at FOSSE 7; remainder of battery at LIERES. Lieut. McALISTER & LEWIS went up to VERMELLES with right section D/68 R.F.A.	1
VERMELLES	" 4		Lieut. SCROGGIE attached to B.A.C. Lieut. WILLIAMS with left section went up to VERMELLES at 10 a.m. Fired 101 rounds at 10 midnight for a barrage behind a mine exploded by us near the German QUARRIES.	
	" 10		2/Lieuts PRICE, WILLIAMS, & LEWIS with right section returned to LIERES. 2/Lieuts McALISTER with left section returned to LIERES.	
LIERES	" 11		Major COTTER & Lieut McALISTER with 4 signallers went up to FOSSE 7.	
	" 14		Lieut WILLIAMS with left section took over from one section of D/73.	
FOSSE 7	" 15		Major COTTER and Lieut. McALISTER with 5 men to the Lone Howitzer in CHALK PIT.	
	" 16		Lieut WILLIAMS took a detachment of 5 men to FOSSE 7 to take over remaining section of D/73.	
	" 17?		Lieut PRICE & LEWIS came up to FOSSE 7. Usual desultory firing.	
	" 23		Lieut WILLIAMS a detachment returned to battery from the Lone Howitzer. Lieut. McALISTER rel. up to Lone Howitzer.	
	" 27		Heavy bombardment of battery position from 5 a.m. to 1 p.m. with Lachrymatory shells, 4.2"s, 5.9"s, and 8" gas attack. Lieut. McALISTER and detachment returned from CHALK PIT suffering from gas poisoning after a futile attempt on the part of Lieut. McALISTER to destroy the gun. & Gunner MEDLICOTT was shot through the head and killed while attempting to leave the CHALK PIT. Lieut PRICE took a fresh detachment up to CHALK PIT in the evening.	

WAR DIARY
INTELLIGENCE SUMMARY

Army Form C. 2118.

Page II

Place	Date	Hour	Summary of Events and Information	Remarks and references to Appendices
FOSSE 7	April 28		All quiet during the day. "S.O.S. gas" alarm at 9 p.m. Proved to be false.	
	" 29		Gas attack from direction of CHALK PIT at 3.45 a.m. and for direction of HULLUCH at 3.50 a.m. Germans seemed to be using a new gas which caused very heavy casualties to the infantry. Our artillery fire caused the enemy to evacuate their front line trenches over a front of 700 yards. There was no infantry attack after the gas. Situation was normal at 5.45 a.m. Lieut. PRICE and detachment returned from CHALK PIT having been driven out by gas. Driver R.A. BOND was sent to hospital suffering from gas poisoning. Sgt. CARRINGTON was slightly wounded in hand.	
	" 30		All quiet on front. Desultory shelling of FOSSE 7. 89 Battery was attached to LEFT GROUP from 10 a.m. today. Special shoot by order of group on POSEN CRATERS at 3 p.m. Corporal A.E. WALKER slightly wounded - thigh.	

J.B. Arbuthnot Lt-A
OC D/1/2 RFA

BAC/77th B# RFA

Army Form C. 2118

WAR DIARY
or
INTELLIGENCE SUMMARY
(Erase heading not required.)

Instructions regarding War Diaries and Intelligence Summaries are contained in F.S. Regs., Part II. and the Staff Manual respectively. Title Pages will be prepared in manuscript.

Place	Date	Hour	Summary of Events and Information	Remarks and references to Appendices
Lières	4.4.16		Lt J.R. SCROGGIE R.F.A temporarily attached from D Battery. 2Lt GOAN & returned from J.M. Course	
Lières	7.4.16 to 9.4.16		Divisional Route March BELLERY- AVCITY au BOIS - OUY. 7e 77th Bob R.F.A was billeted at WESTREHAM. The billets were good.	
	8.4.16		2Lt- GOING, Cpl JENKINS and Gnr GRIMES went to Trench Mortar battery Y16	
Lières	10.4.16		2Lt ROBERTON attached to Crumm from A Battery 77th RFA R.F.A on return from T. M. course & hospital.	
Lières	11.4.16		2Lt T.L DAVIES + 5NCOs + 1 man proceeded to 73 R.A.C for a course of instruction un til 15 inst. No 49449 Gnr SIMPSON, No 84361 Gnr WINDSOR (both attached)- Gnr 70421 Gnr HENDERSON went to Y 15 T.M battery. 2Lt ROBERTON went into Hospital No 6 Casualty Clearing Stn at LILLERS	
Lières	14.4.16			
Lières	15.4.16		No 32239 Gnr CUTTS, No 17221 Gnr WILTSHIRE No 14713 Gnr COCKLIN, No 9722 Gnr HUSSEY, No 2 6024 Gnr LETTON (all attached) went to X 15 T.M. Battery	

1875 Wt. W593/826 1,000,000 4/15 J.B.C. & A. A.D.S.S./Forms/C. 2118.

WAR DIARY or INTELLIGENCE SUMMARY

Army Form C. 2118

Place	Date	Hour	Summary of Events and Information	Remarks and references to Appendices
LIERES	13.4.16		No 69963 Gnr KILLOW, No 31791 Gnr DUFFIELD, No 69838 Bdr STEEL returned from course with Y15 T.M. battery	
LIERES	14.4.16		No 71409 Gnr SULLY and Gnr 70726 Gnr SIMMONS left for a Trench Mortar Course at the Trench Mortar School	
LIERES	16.4.16		S' VENANT. The BAC 77th Bde R.F.A. left with the remainder of the Divisional Artillery to relieve the 15th Division Artillery	
VERQUIN	16.4.16 7.30pm		The BAC 77th Bde RFA arrived at VERQUIN.	
VERQUIN	17.4.16		The BAC 97 th Bde RFA started supply by ammunition to the Bde wagon lines.	
VERQUIN	20.4.16 4.30 pm		Lt J.R. SCROGIE proceeded in charge of an R.A. working party of 12 men + 1 NCO supplied from the Batteries under the direction of 224 Records P56 R.E.C.E. to LOOS. 16 went on Trench Mortar emplace- ments. At LOOS a wagon shook in 15 open road + was shelled by percussion shrapnel, all the mules being wounded, 2Lt ROBERTS R.E. + two sappers were wounded. No casualties to the Bde working party. The wounded were attended to by Lt Scrogie, and the wagon was then manhandled into LOOS.	

WAR DIARY or INTELLIGENCE SUMMARY

Army Form C. 2118

(Erase heading not required.)

Place	Date	Hour	Summary of Events and Information	Remarks and references to Appendices
VERQUIN	20.4.16	4:30pm	Lt. J.R. SCROGGIE proceeded with 11 men + 2 NCO's of Mr. B.A.C. in a wagon to Bde HQRS. Lt J.R. SCROGGIE then had charge of 25 men R.A. under the directions of the R.E. 156 Co. Work was carried on through the night & the party arrived back at Bde HQRS at 4.45 am on 22nd inst.	
VERQUIN	23.4.16		No 91409 Gnr SULLY and No 70726 Gnr SIMMONS returned from the Trench Mortar Course at the Trench Mortar School, ST VENANT. Lt. T.F. Davies proceeded to Bde Hdqtrs with 1 NCO + 7 men of the BAC. He then had charge of 20 men R.A under the direction of a Sgt of R.E. 156 Co. The work was completed. T.M. emplacements at HULLUCH. No casualties. It being the returning of Bde Hdqtrs at 4.0 am on 24th inst. the party returned to the BAC.	
	27.4.16		The BAC had its greatest demand for ammunition on this day. They sent up 4126 rounds to the Batteries. The Bde Commander complimented the BAC upon their despatch.	
	28.4.16		Bdr. James 19970 was posted to Bde Hdqtrs to replace a casualty. Dr. Marshall 43580 was promoted Bombardier vice Bdr James 19970.	
	29.4.16		A.J.R. Scroggie was transferred to D/177 and Lt G.H. Roberton was posted to the BAC upon evacuation from hospital.	
	30.4.16			

T.F. Davies Lt RFA
77th BAC.

WAR DIARY or INTELLIGENCE SUMMARY.

Army Form C. 2118.

77 RFA Vol 4

Place	Date	Hour	Summary of Events and Information	Remarks and references to Appendices
FOSSE 6	1/5/16	10am	The GROUP system came into being. Pursuant to this each Brigade has been handled as a Tactical Unit under its own Brigade Commander. On this line 2 Groups a Right & a Left were formed. Right Group under command of Lieut Col H.M. Thomas to which A/77 and D/77 were attached. Left Group under Col. H.F. McKenzie C.M.G. to which B/77 was attached. Lieuts Badcock and Chanctres were posted to the Brigade and sent to B Battery and the T.A.C. respectively.	
	1/5/16	3pm	B/77 acting in reference to a request from Inf 12th HQ opened fire on "POZEN CRATER" with good effect.	
			Enemy's observation balloons up from daybreak and fire appears to be directed from them.	
FOSSE 6	2/5/16		On the whole a quiet period - with occasional shelling fraternally at FOSSE 7 by the enemy with 5.9"s & 4.2". Enemy usually shells in the early morning and late in the afternoon. During a more favourable light conditions in the afternoon the bulk of our shelling takes place then.	
FOSSE 6	4/5/16			
	9/5/16			
FOSSE 6	9/5/16	4pm	A quiet morning - later on the enemy heavily bombarded VERMELLES, PHILOSOPHE, FOSSE 3, FOSSE 7, + MAROC. Fire was intense on these positions between 4-3pm + 7.30pm. Salvoes coming over in quick succession with TEAR GAS shells. No casualties were reported but a vigorous shelling of the enemies front lines	

77th (How) Brigade R.F.A.

Army Form C. 2118.

WAR DIARY
or
INTELLIGENCE SUMMARY
(Erase heading not required.)

Place	Date	Hour	Summary of Events and Information	Remarks and references to Appendices
FOSSE 6	13/5/16, 14/5/16		Normally quiet days — very little doing	
FOSSE 6	17/5/16		Reconnaissance, extending over several days, was carried out by the Brigade Commander, Adjutant & Orderly Officer for the purpose of reinforcing the 16th Divisional Front with a whole Divisional Artillery.	
FOSSE 6	23/5/16		Lieut Lewis A/77 joined the 16th Divisional Artillery School on a course of instruction.	
FOSSE 6	24/5/16		Information received of the impending breakup of the Brigade Ammunition Column to be replaced by a new echelon of the B.A.C. still commanded by Major Heather, present B.A.C. Commander. Major Heather & Lieut Christmas were notes to transfer from the R.F.A. to R.E. Lieut Davis (notes) from B.A.C. to C/77. B.S.M. Richards 77 Transferred to B.A.C. vice B.S.M. Harper B.A.C/77 to D/77.	
FOSSE 6	28/5/16		5 Chargers, 3 Riders & 34 L.D horses were received from the B.A.C. on the upkeep of Kit Unif & were allotted to the 4 Batteries & Brigade HQ	
FOSSE 6	30/5/16		The Brigade Head Quarters were shelled by the Germans in retaliation for the shelling of their advanced positions by 9.2" guns. About 6 4.1 Guns shells fell in quick succession in the house & garden occupied by the Officers mess. There were 3 direct hits on the house, but no casualties to Officers or servants who were all present at the time —	

Army Form C. 2118.

WAR DIARY
or
INTELLIGENCE SUMMARY.
(Erase heading not required.)

Instructions regarding War Diaries and Intelligence Summaries are contained in F.S. Regs., Part II. and the Staff Manual respectively. Title pages will be prepared in manuscript.

Place	Date	Hour	Summary of Events and Information	Remarks and references to Appendices
MAROC	1.5.16		Quiet day on our front. Lt W.H. Gros joins, attached for 14 days course of instruction	
	2.5.16		" " " " A few 5.9 fell into Paris III at 7.40 am and actually four at 12.5th 1	
	3.5.16		Nothing of importance. Gas alarm in the evening which turned out to be false	
	4.5.16		Nothing unusual. The enemy shell dome 7 & LOOS crassier a good deal each day. We	
	5.5.16		do a certain amount of retaliation his return 98 rounds per gun to 125 C.T. drain	
	6.5.16		and dump to 156 at the guns and 52 at waggon line.	
	7.5.16			
	8.5.16			
	9.5.16		Very quiet day about 4.30 pm put over 2 x 5.9 on the Maroc Ch or near 110.b.d.4 pm seemed	
			to kill C.T. Twaddle. First casualty in the battery.	
	10.5.16		nil	
	11.5.16		4.5 pm very heavy enemy bombardment of trenches in vicinity of Hohenzollern. Enemy also	
			fired some 7.7 a lot and any of our guns which might have been left position during	
			enemy attack failed to fire. No retaliation	
	12.5.16		nil	
	13.5.16		nil. Waggon line inspected by Bde Commander.	
	14.5.16		nil	
	15.5.16		nil	
	16.5.16		Hostile H.A. active throughout day on our gun position	
	17.5.16		nil	
	18.5.16		nil	
	19.5.16		Shoot 7 shells from 2.30 to 3.40 with 5.9	
	20.5.16		nil	
	21.5.16		Fired 25 rounds at stone in LONS RAISÉ and 50 rounds at 4 points entering front line to enemy taken	
			Some fighting near Vimy & other enemy rear lines point which are not fired are ? flat out.	
	22.5.16		nil	
	23.5.16			
	24.5.16			
	25.5.16		Did gun registration in the "Triangle" but first 6 R gun taken over 37 rounds.	
	26.5.16		29 rounds	

Army Form C. 2118.

WAR DIARY
or
INTELLIGENCE SUMMARY.
(Erase heading not required.)

Instructions regarding War Diaries and Intelligence Summaries are contained in F.S. Regs., Part II. and the Staff Manual respectively. Title pages will be prepared in manuscript.

Place	Date	Hour	Summary of Events and Information	Remarks and references to Appendices
MAROC	27.5.16		Enemy shell N MAROC with 5.9 at 5 this afternoon from 2.15 till 4.30. They hit Schoolhouse O.P. and four several hits. The Battery. No damage or casualties.	
	28.5.16		Intense bombardment of the trenches near CHAPEL PIT north of 27/4pm. S.9. Our attached in Russia trenches. Enemy opened at 7.20. He got back more than he sent over.	
	29.5.16		Nil.	
	30.5.16		Enemy shelled N MAROC with 4.2. Three or four fell in Battery. No damage	
	31.5.16		ditto	

[signature] Captain
Comdg A/M

2353 Wt. W2544/1454 700,000 5/15 D.D. & L. A.D.S.S./Forms/C. 2118.

Army Form C. 2118

WAR DIARY
or
INTELLIGENCE SUMMARY

(Erase heading not required.)

B. BATTERY - 77th (How) Bde. R.F.A.

Instructions regarding War Diaries and Intelligence Summaries are contained in F. S. Regs., Part II. and the Staff Manual respectively. Title Pages will be prepared in manuscript.

Place	Date	Hour	Summary of Events and Information	Remarks and references to Appendices
FOSSE.7	30/6/16	10.A.M	B.77th (How) Bde. became attached to "LEFT-GROUP" (182nd Bde. Hd. Qrs.) for Tactical purposes only, remaining under the administrative control of 77th (How) Bde. Hd. Qrs.	
	1st May 3.0 p.m.		By request of Inf. B.E. Hd. Qrs., fire was opened on "POSEN CRATER" - outline of CRATER alone in appearance and SUPPORT & COMMUNICATION TRENCH behind a good deal knocked about. The wind was rather left and range rather long for close shooting - 57 Rnds of B.X were fired.	
	2nd May 5.45 a.m.		Enemy shelled FOSSE.7. and VICTORIA STATION with 5.9" How. Dispersed fire in reply and pairs coming from direction of ANNAY - CITE ST-AUGUSTE & SOUTH of VENDIN. Observation balloons up since daybreak and fire seems to be directed from them. A quiet night on our front.	
	" " 2.35 p.m.		Fire opened on working party at H.20.C.6.4. to 6.4½. - Working Party dispersed, several times and a quantity of material thrown up. tench hit	
	3rd May 4.10 p.m.		By request of Inf. B.E. Hd. Qrs. fire was opened in retaliation of enemy shelling of our front & reserve trenches at G.24.B.44. - our fire was also directed on H.13.G.82.58. - Redoubt and Communication Trenches and a fortified House.	
	4th to 9th May		Quiet days on our front, but slight shelling with 5.9" & 4.2" of FOSSE.7. especially the POWER-STATION - MINE WORKS & QUALITY-STREET is taking place daily, usually early morning and late in the afternoon.	

Army Form C. 2118

WAR DIARY
or
INTELLIGENCE SUMMARY

B. BATTERY. 77th (How) Bde. R.G.A.

(Erase heading not required.)

Place	Date	Hour	Summary of Events and Information	Remarks and references to Appendices
FOSSE.7.	10th May	3-20	Retaliated for intermittent shelling on our communication trenches, by firing 25 Rds. B.X on German Battery at H.14.B.0.6. Previous to this, at about 12.45 p.m. the enemy sent over several rounds of P.15.9 cracks & 4.2" from direction of St. BENIFONTAINE & VENDIN. This fire was evidently drawn by careless movement of troops above parapet.	
		5-35.	28 Rnd. B.X fired on CHATEAU and Communication Trench in H.14.C.½.4.	
	11th May	4-15.	After a fairly quiet morning, the enemy commenced shelling VERMELLES with 5.9"& 4.2". The fire was for some time almost entirely concentrated on VERMELLES, but gradually developed into an intense Bombardment of the Batteries at VERMELLES, PHILOSOPHE, FOSSE B. FOSSE 7. and MAROC. From about 4.45 to about 7-30 p.m. Salvos came often in quick succession and a number of "TEAR GAS" shells were dropped in our position. Several shells fell into the Compound, two dropped on the site of new GUNPITS. But no material damage was done and there were no casualties to report. All was quiet again. We replied with several salvos in nighttime.	
		8-15.		
	12th	7-20 a.m.	Fired 8 rounds on REDOUBT & Communication Trench H.20.☐ - 5 direct His were obtained and a quantity of material thrown up.	
	13th to 16th May		Uneventful and abnormally quiet days on our front	

Army Form C. 2118

WAR DIARY
or
INTELLIGENCE SUMMARY
(Erase heading not required.)

B. BATTERY. 77ᵈ (How) Bde. R.F.A.

Instructions regarding War Diaries and Intelligence Summaries are contained in F.S. Regs., Part II. and the Staff Manual respectively. Title Pages will be prepared in manuscript.

Place	Date	Hour	Summary of Events and Information	Remarks and references to Appendices
FOSSE-7	17ᵗʰ (&) 18ᵗʰ May	10 p.m to 10 pm	Between 10 p.m. 17ᵗʰ and 10 p.m. 18ᵗʰ May Fosse 7. was vacated by this Unit and a position taken over from the 40ᵗʰ (How) Battery R.F.A. at SOUTH MAROC.	
SOUTH MAROC	18ᵃ	10 P.M.	390 Rds of B.X were taken over from 40ᵗʰ Bty and during the day a number of R.Os were fixed for the purpose Registration. Gun platforms were rebuilt and improved, new lines laid out."	
		9.30	Relief completed. Unit attached to "Right Group" for tactical purposes, but still remain for administration under 77ᵗʰ Bde.	
	20 May	2.30 to 6 pm	During the afternoon a number of rounds were fired on Enemy's front and support Trenches in M.5.R.21 - N.F.R.5.P.½ - H.31.B.53½ - H.5.R.21 - N.F.R.5.P.½ for purpose of effect & registration	
	21ˢᵗ - 23ʳᵈ		Firing for Registration purpose continued by order of "Right Group"	
	24 to 28ᵃ		Quiet days on our front. – Working Parties are detailed daily for improvement at O.P. detachment employed in strengthening & improving Gun pits & concealment.	

1875. Wt. W593/826 1,000,000 4/15 J.B.C. & A. A.D.S.S./Forms/C. 2118.

Army Form C. 2118

WAR DIARY
or
INTELLIGENCE SUMMARY
(Erase heading not required.)

B. BATTERY - 77th (How) Bde. R.F.A

Place	Date	Hour	Summary of Events and Information	Remarks and references to Appendices
SOUTH MAROC	29/5/16	4.55 p.m	Orders were received from "RIGHT GROUP" to open fire FRONT LINE TRENCHES & TRENCH JUNCTIONS and a number of rounds were fired on M.5.B.74.4 - M.8.C.2.9 & M.11.B.C.4½ - A number of Targets were registered.	
		6.55 p.m.	26. RND J. B.X. were fired on SNIPERS Hd. Gates in M.6.C.4½.4½.	
	30"	9.55 a.m.	Fired 16 Rds on front line Trench in _____ to be known right up in the air and a quantity of material was thrown up. Several direct hits were obtained, one German was seen ____	

General

No. 13334. Sgt. Hinton.J.J. & No. 13376. Gnr. Thomas.E. were awarded a CERTIFICATE OF HONOUR for devotion to duty and bravery displayed on the morning of the 27th April 1916, in that they, after the Gun Pit had been struck by a GAS-SHELL, put in three new BREECH MECHANISM and kept on serving their Gun.

HEALTH & GENERAL CONDITIONS

During the latter part of the month the percentage of minor accidents and illness was rather above the average and in the 3rd week a total of Q.R.C.O.s & men were in Hospital, chiefly suffering from kicks & cuts & strained ankles. They all were eventually evacuated to Casualty Clearing Stations. A total absence of ordinary illness is to be noted, which may be attributed to Excellent Latrine arrangements and a good water supply.

Horses

Very little sickness amongst Horses, but 2 died during the month from Colic. There is a total absence of Skin disease.

Establishment - The establishment was increased by 1 officer, 1 Batman & 1 Riding Horse.

Army Form C. 2118

WAR DIARY
or
INTELLIGENCE SUMMARY

(Erase heading not required.) B. BATTERY. 77th (How) Bde. R.G.A

Place	Date	Hour	Summary of Events and Information	Remarks and references to Appendices
SOUTH HAM			ESTABLISHMENT Continued.	
			On the 25th May. the establishment of Horses was again reduced by 2 and 2 additional Bicycles taken on charge.	
			1 Chayer & 1 Rider were received during the month, to make up deficiencies caused by evacuation etc.	
			2/Lt. B.H. Lane. R.F.A. Posted to this unit 23-4-16	
			" " " " " to B.A.C. 22-5-16	

O.S. Mustard
Major. R.G.A
COMDG. B. 77th (HOW.) BDE. R.F.A.

WAR DIARY or INTELLIGENCE SUMMARY

Army Form C. 2118

C. Battery — 74th Bde.

Summary of Events and Information for MAY 1916

Place	Date	Hour	Summary of Events and Information	Remarks and references to Appendices
PHILOSOPHE	1-5-16		Quiet day.	
	2-5-16		Battery position shelled twice heavily by 5.9" shell from 7 AM to 9 AM. No. 13857 Gnr. E. Jones was hit in the face by a fragment of shell. Only other casualty was the water cart which was also evacuated. False gas alarm.	
	3-5-16	2 A.M.	12 men from DAC were posted to the battery.	
	5-5-16		A few 5.9" shell near the guns. No damage done.	
	7-5-16		Nothing happened at Bty position till afternoon when the 5 guns were heavily shelled by 5.9" shell. No. 139549 J Donnelly was killed by a fragment of shell which struck him in the neck whilst he was running for cover. A dug-out in corner 7 communication was destroyed by a direct hit. The O.P. at Fosse 3 was shelled during the day by an H.V. 6" gun.	
	11-5-16	4 P.M.	A fairly heavy attack was launched by the enemy on our front heavily shelled especially with gas shell. The battery fired 82 rounds from 3 J Fosse 8 & 6 Kellock. The battery position was very to fire. Futher R. Wilson 50345 was badly affected by gas in C broken in by a shell, also the O.P. was damaged. Taken to hospital. C's dug out was Gun pit was afterwards taken to hospital. was reported the following night No. 130. The battery fired 70 A counter attack took place between 4 P.M & 7 P.M. The battery fired 70 rounds to support it on hostile Bty 130. The enemy did not retaliate much behind the support lines	
	14-5-16			
	17-5-16		Considerable activity 6.30 PM onwards Bty fired 57 rounds in support of our attack. Not much retaliation in our direction.	
	18-5-16		Capt. Arnold left on 10 days leave.	

Army Form C. 2118

WAR DIARY
or
INTELLIGENCE SUMMARY
(Erase heading not required.)

C. Bty 47th Bde.

Place	Date	Hour	Summary of Events and Information	Remarks and references to Appendices
PHILOSOPHE	21.5.16		NOEUX LES MINES shelled. One round fell in wagon lines - no damage done.	
	22.5.16		2 Cr. T.L. Davis was posted to the Battery from B.A.C.	
	23.5.16		Considerable activity in Souchez sector. 7.20.PM. Battery stood to, but was not called on to fire.	
	24.5.16		MSC 13 & MSC 25½, MSC 36 registered by order from Group 6 from Loyelan O.P. with a view to a "stoof". 28 Rounds fired.	
	26.5.16		Comm. in chief sent congratulations to R.A. on 200th anniversary of foundation. 31 rounds fired to complete registration of previous day.	
	27.5.16		16 Rounds fired at OPo on Fosse 8.	
	28.5.16		1 man on leave.	
	29.5.16		Pte. Arnold returned from leave. 16 Ran fired.	
	30.5.16		"Stoof" mentioned on 25th inst. cancelled.	

W Hurdy Capt
O/C C/D. RFA.

Army Form C. 2118.

D/77th (How) Bde R.F.A.

WAR DIARY
or
INTELLIGENCE SUMMARY
(Erase heading not required.)

Instructions regarding War Diaries and Intelligence Summaries are contained in F.S. Regs. Part II. and the Staff Manual respectively. Title pages will be prepared in manuscript.

Place	Date	Hour	Summary of Events and Information	Remarks and references to Appendices
FOSSE 7	4-5-16		Registered a new night-line for No 4 gun at H.25.A.8.6.	
"	11-5-16	4 pm to 7.45 pm	Enemy shelled the FOSSE 7 & surrounding batteries with shells of all calibres using H.E.'s & lachrymatory & asphyxiating shells. Cover of No 4 gunpit was struck with a weapon. All wires were cut.	
"	12-5-16	4 pm	We strafed POSEN CRATER at request of infantry. Considerable damage was done. Sap & dugout was hit with a pipsqueak but no damage was done.	
"	16-5-16		New gunpit commenced to receive a new gun in place of the LONE HOWITZER handed over to 15th D.A.	
"	19-5-16		New gun brought up & put into the pit. This gun become No 2 gun.	
"	5-15 pm to 8 pm		Enemy shelled FOSSE 7 with 5·9 lachrymatory & H.E. shells from direction of ANNAY. About 200 rds were fired at No damage was done to the battery. "Lieut W.H. WADSWORTH was on 3 days leave to JUERQUIN.	
"	20-5-16 1 a.m.		Enemy shelled QUALITY STREET with about 100 5·9s from direction of LENS. We registered new gun a night-line for new gun.	
"	21-5-16	4pm to 9pm	Enemy shelled FOSSE 7 with 5·9" lachrymatory & H.E. from direction of LENS. About 800 rounds fired.	
"	28-5-16		"LIEUT H.R.PRICE went on leave. 12th D.A. came up to replace 16th D.A. during the night.	
"	29-5-16 12 Noon		Enemy shelled FOSSE 7 with 5·9s from direction of LENS. Shells all went 200 yds over battery & no damage was done.	
"	30-5-16		No 4's dugout had a direct hit with a 4·2. Roof kept shell out & no damage was done.	

T. Speers, Major R.F.A.
Commanding D/77th Bde R.F.A.

77th Brigade R.F.A.

Army Form C. 2118.

WAR DIARY
or
INTELLIGENCE SUMMARY.
(Erase heading not required.)

Vol 5
XVI
77. R.F.A.
June

Place	Date	Hour	Summary of Events and Information	Remarks and references to Appendices
FOSSE 6	June 2nd	—	The 77th (Howitzer) Brigade ceased to exist on this date and Batteries were reformed in Brigades under the new reorganization scheme, which provides 3 18/pr. Batteries and 1 4.5" (How) Battery for each Brigade. In accordance with this, the 77th Brigade was formed on 2nd June and composed as under:— A/77 (former D/77) Battery Commander — Capt R.B. Neve 6 Officers 132 Other Ranks 125 Horses B/77 (former D/180) Battery Commander — Major Sir C.S. Hope Dunbar 5 Officers 131 Other Ranks 124 Horses C/77 (former D/182) Battery Commander. Capt H.J. Glendinning 5 Officers 135 Other Ranks 124 Horses D/77 (former C/77) Battery Commander. Capt W. Arnold 5 Officers 135 Other Ranks 123 Horses	

Army Form C. 2118.

WAR DIARY
or
INTELLIGENCE SUMMARY.
(Erase heading not required.)

Instructions regarding War Diaries and Intelligence Summaries are contained in F. S. Regs., Part II. and the Staff Manual respectively. Title pages will be prepared in manuscript.

Place	Date	Hour	Summary of Events and Information	Remarks and references to Appendices
FOSSE 6	12/6/16	—	A/77 continued to be attached to the H.R. Group as Counter battery but comes under 77th Brigade control for administration & Discipline.	
			The former 77th (How) Brigade H.Q. became the Brigade H.Q. of the 77th Brigade.	
			The Batteries of the 77th (How) Brigade were distributed as follows A/77 became B/182 – B/77 became C/77 became D/77	
	14/6/16		The Right Section of B/178 of the 40th Division was attached for instruction to B/77 from this date.	
			B/77 reported one gun (4.5" How) with defective rifling. 20 Rounds were fired on a hostile gun emplacement at H.20 a.5.0 by order of the I.O.M for the purpose of testing the rifling.	
FOSSE 6	25-27/6/16		All the Batteries of the Brigade took part in the bombardment of special points in the enemy's lines e.g. Trench mortars, O.P.s, communication trenches and road junctions.	
FOSSE 6	28/6/16		The 8th Leicesters carried out a successful raid during the night, killing a large number of the enemy, and bringing back one prisoner, a Saxon attached to the Prussian Guard	

77th Brigade RFA

Army Form C. 2118.

WAR DIARY
or
INTELLIGENCE SUMMARY.
(Erase heading not required.)

Place	Date	Hour	Summary of Events and Information	Remarks and references to Appendices
FOT E 6	28/27/6/16		C/77 took part with other Batteries of the Right Group of 16th D.A. in covering this raid - by bombarding the enemy's front line & subsequently turned a barrage. The Barrage was kept up for some 3 hours. Some 1100 rounds were fired by this Battery - Enemy's retaliation was weak and inaccurate. C/77 engaged 2 enemy trench mortars and silenced both	
FOT E 6	30/6/16		2/7/16	

S.J.F. Taylor Lt Col
Comdt 77 "A" RFA

WAR DIARY
INTELLIGENCE SUMMARY

Army Form C. 2118

June 1916

Place	Date	Hour	Summary of Events and Information	Remarks and references to Appendices
Philosophe	1/6/16		Registered two guns on a hostile gun emplacement at H.2.a.0.5. which was under course of construction (obtained several direct hits and was entirely rendered useless & very conspicuous). Davies & two Barney went to 77th bde Hd.qts. to temporarily act as orderly officers.	
	2/6/16	12.25 P.M	A hostile 5.9 gun shelled area around G.14.D.1.5. Shelling lasted 2 hrs and was fairly intense.	
	3/6/16		Marked out and commenced to dig, in rear of the Gun position, a trench 100ft long and 8ft deep for the purpose of burying cable.	
	5/6/16		3 med 14 Rds on pt. H.2.a.b b.8.	
	8/6/16		Coroys du Rutoire (G.14.c&d) was heavily bombarded with hostile 5.9's & 4.2's. Ag. the nearest & only one occasional Rd. fell within our position. Several casualties were recorded within the position. Some shelling was Downn...	
	9/6/16		The left section of D/176 & the 40th Div. became attached to his B'ty for Instruction	
	11/6/16		Fired 16 Rds on the Redoubt.	
	12/6/16			
	14/6/16		The Right sect'n of D/178 the 40th Div became attached to this B'ty for Instruction. The Right sec'n erected over head cover for the horses at 10 waggon Lines.	

WAR DIARY or INTELLIGENCE SUMMARY

Army Form C. 2118

June 1916.

Place	Date	Hour	Summary of Events and Information	Remarks and references to Appendices
Philosophe	14/6/16		Fired 20 Rounds in Hostile Gun Emplacement at H.20.d.5.0. These rounds were fired at the order of the I.O.M. for the purpose of testing No #3 Gun. The rifling of this gun was defective.	
	15/6/16		"C" Sub-section Gun (479 C.O.W) was sent to the Ordnance workshop at Bethune for repairs. Fired 65 Rounds by way of Retaliation for the attacked Battery.	
	16/6/16 17/6/16		#2 Squadron R.F.C. established a wireless station at this Battery's position. We were ordered to send 30 men weekly to D/185 to build gun pits for them. This expedient was adopted at was no wagon lines.	
	18/6/16		Fired 22 Rds on Point 14 bis. H.20.A.5.0, H.20.C.7.7.X These rounds were fired for the purpose of destroying the attached Battery.	
	19/6/16		Fired 16 Rds on houses in M.31.b.6.5.	
	20/6/16		Fired 17 Rds on H.26.C.2.5 and H.20.A.5.0 for the purpose of destruction & attacked Battery.	
	22/6/16		Horse (&TD) died of Colic. Fired 8 Rds on pt. H.20.a.9.1 and 8 Rds on H.32.A.	
	24/6/16		Fired 10 Rds on a Suspected Gun position at H.20.c.3.8.	
	25/6/16		Rcd. Gun 667 C.O.W. from the Ordnance workshop in place of (479 C.O.W) which was taken away on the 15th.	
	28/6/16		Fired 56 Rds on Support trenches in accordance with orders received from 6" H.A Group and was now working with the 43rd Group. Capt the 6" H.A Group. W.Arnold Cpt 2/77

Army Form C. 2118

"C" Battery 77th Bde R.F.A (late D/182) — WAR DIARY or INTELLIGENCE SUMMARY

Instructions regarding War Diaries and Intelligence Summaries are contained in F.S. Regs., Part II. and the Staff Manual respectively. Title Pages will be prepared in manuscript.

(Erase heading not required.)

Place	Date	Hour	Summary of Events and Information	Remarks and references to Appendices
MAROC (M26.53½ Sheet 36c SW)	June 1		A quiet day and very little shooting done — a few rounds were fired in retaliation (relieving HARRISON'S CRATER — (21A + 51AX)	/18
	2		A few working parties dispersed and a sniper's post located and destroyed (57A and 106AX)	/16, /17
	3		nil	
	4		Engaged an aeroplane target — observation O.K — wireless now installed in battery telephone pit H.Q	
	5		nil	
	6		nil	
	7		Nos 5 working parties were engaged in Hill 70 and dispersed — 3 G.P targets engaged but not very successfully — a little retaliation for enemy shelling (25A + 3s-7X)	/15
	8		Retaliation only (30 rounds fired)	
	9		2 G.P Targets Engaged — 6060 O.K — a quiet day (112 A + 10 AX)	/12
	10–13		Retaliation 56 rounds may hrs (Enemy quiet and not aggressive)	/13
	14		Zone often shifted slightly etc from to flank of B/182 battery to come in in its right line — Zone was from HARRISON'S CRATER on the right to end of LOOS CRASSIER on its left.	
	15		NSW line registered and zero house — (65A + 50AX)	/12
	16		A few working parties dispersed from near crest of Hill 70 —	/11
	17		nil	
	18		nil	
	19		3 working parties dispersed from Hill 70 —	/10
	20		2 working parties dispersed from Hill 70 — ;	
	21		A heavy trench mortar was engaged and silenced — very difficult to locate in maps as the trench maps are very inaccurate —	/13
	22–23		nil	
	24		Bombarded enemy O.P's and suspected O.P's — Enemy retaliation feeble and return trench to and and	/13
	25		Bombardment works and trench shots in enemy territory, also M.T and communications	/19
	26		Bombarded Enemy communication trenches, works and billets during daylight	/18
	27			

1875 Wt. W593/826 1,000,000 4/15 J.B.C. & A. A.D.S.S./Forms/C. 2118.

C/ 77th Brigade (War D/182)
R.F.A.

Army Form C. 2118

WAR DIARY
or
INTELLIGENCE SUMMARY
(Erase heading not required.)

II

Instructions regarding War Diaries and Intelligence Summaries are contained in F. S. Regs., Part II. and the Staff Manual respectively. Title Pages will be prepared in manuscript.

Place	Date	Hour	Summary of Events and Information	Remarks and references to Appendices
	Jan 26		A quiet day and practically nothing done.	VR
	26-27		On 8th Lancers carried out a successful raid during tonight — they killed a large number of Germans but only brought back one prisoner — a Saxon abstracted to the Russian Front — unfortunately he was wounded whilst being brought in and was brought on and then premature[?], and his wish [illegible] up for some 3 hours and a rate of battery fire. The barrage was kept up for some 3 hours and a rate of [illegible] ten to seconds. Some two rounds went short. Enemy retaliation weakly and seemed quite lost and not appear to know himself to return against the barrage. Bombarded enemy OP's — Enemy ammunition dump — Enemy spirit —	VR
	28 & 29			
	29 & 30		Engaged 2 enemy trench mortars, both silenced. Bombarded enemy OP's — tried to counter-battery support enemy attack by 1st Div on our right. This seemed badly managed and an even heavily punished — a snow barrage was maintained on the left of the attack but practically none on the right —	VR

[signature]
OC/C/77

Army Form C. 2118

WAR DIARY
or
INTELLIGENCE SUMMARY
(Erase heading not required.)

B/77 RFA
for D/180

Place	Date	Hour	Summary of Events and Information	Remarks and references to Appendices
G.33.a.4.5.	1/6/16.	—	The morale of the men both of wagon line and at guns is splendid, and unflagging energy is shown by all ranks in digging and completing new dug-outs.	
	2/6/16.	—	To-day this Battery B/180, becomes B/77, though still under the tactical command of the 180th Bde. Registration of some lost points by aeroplane observation was attempted, but 52 rds. of AX were expended with no results. Working parties were dispersed.	
	3/6/16.	—	Retaliatory fire was opened on trenches in BOIS HUGO, by order from front. 16 A were expended. Working parties dispersed.	
	8/6/16	—	On this day no less than 40 A were expended on retaliatory fire — the then being active on our front support lines with 4.2"s.	
	9/6/16.	—	10 A were expended in registering new night lines — orders by group – Sups Y5, Y6, Y7, Y8.	
	10/6/16.	—	26 A were expended for retaliation for enemy trench mortars. The shooting was good, which trench mortars ceased.	
	19/6/16	—	26 Rds, 4A, 20 AX, were expended in registering "Defend LOOS", by order of Group. This was done from A/180's O.P. Laying was good.	
	20/6/16.	—	Working parties at H.3.R, a, w. 9. — dispersed. A great deal of work appears to be doing at this spot. Probably an emplacement for exts.	
	20/6/16.	—	Working parties at this same spot continually dispersed; several casualties inflicted, yet work continues.	
	23/6/16.	—	The work now appears to be a field gun emplacement with a cement roof, [illegible] to rifle [illegible] but cannot get shells into it.	

WAR DIARY
or
INTELLIGENCE SUMMARY
(Erase heading not required.)

Army Form C. 2118

Place	Date	Hour	Summary of Events and Information	Remarks and references to Appendices
F.32.a.4.5.	24/6/16	—	During the morning 60 AX were shot at outposts O.P. at H.32.a.6.3½. Though the last lot was not actually hit, considerable damage was done to the trench & the head of junction in its immediate vicinity. A repairing party came out as light began to fail. They were dispersed. Work also continued on field gun emplacement at H.32.a.4.8.7., and lines of fire were being laid out with a friend, marked in the twilight with a blue flag. That party was dispersed and a report sent to left front confirming suspicions that this was a Field gun emplacement.	
	25/6/16	—	During the day by order 60 Sc. A.X. were divided between our O.P. & M.G. emplacement at H.25.d.4.4. Two direct hits were obtained on the latter. Enemy were excellent.	
	26/6/16	—	Retaliatory shots were fired in the morning, during today 60 Sc AX were fired at T.M. emplacement at H.31.6.3.95, no more damage being done to trench. Gun AX in range. 2 minutes of 9 gr. negligible. Working party at suspected gun emplacement again dispersed.	
	27/6/16	—	30 Sc. A X at M.G. emplacement at H.25.d.6.4. These fired hits, but this emplacement is too strong to (8 Plns. Sniping the ards few days been 18pdrs. have been able carrying on as before to. prepare by T.M.'s and 18pdrs. have been was to keep the flat turf at night every day all day. the line 18 Pdrs. Rare shots steering to disturb troops upon "C.T's" etc. with a view to annoying the enemy.	

Place	Date	Hour	Summary of Events and Information	Remarks and references to Appendices
G.32.a.b.5.	28/6/16	—	In the early morning i.e. 1 a.m. LOOS WALLAH was subjected to our own but only 5 rounds was used and on three attempts bombardment to which their reply was negligible. For some reason unknown to us any work which our barrage was stopped of the enemy stopping to an hour rendered it.	
—	29/6/16	—	During the day the O.P. at H.32.a.6.3.t. was again the objective. Some fire 63 rds. 4.x being shot, considerable damage being done to the trench.	
—	30/6/16	—	Again today this same O.P. was again bombarded with 52 A.X. 20 A.X. being fired again at O.P. at a.b. in BOIS DE DIX HUIT. a truce was did. It being direct than O.P., which was a stroke of luck at such a range.	

C.D Arfred Dunlan
Major R.F.A.
Comdg B/177 R.F.A.

WAR DIARY

77th Brigade
Royal Field Artillery

1st. July to 31st. July 1916.

VOLUME No. 6

44th Brigade R.F.A.

Army Form C. 2118.

WAR DIARY
or
INTELLIGENCE SUMMARY

(Erase heading not required.)

Place	Date	Hour	Summary of Events and Information	Remarks and references to Appendices
FOSSE 6	1/7/16	-	Quiet day. Heavy gun fire of the great offensive was clearly audible	
	2/7/16	-	Quiet day. Nothing to report	
	3/7/16	-	" " " " "	
	4/7/16	-	" " " " "	
	5/7/16	-	1st Munsters made a raid during night 4/5. B/77 report raid was unsuccessful they had a gun put out of action through trail breaking.	
	6/7/16	-	Temp. Capt. A.H. Corbett, R.F.A. was attached to the Brigade from 16th D.A.C. and has been placed in charge of A/77 Wagon line. Heavy rain fell on B/77 position with 4.2" Hows., he destroyed their splinter-proof outhouse with a direct hit severely injuring 2 men, No 29241 Bombr. May J. and No 29547 Gnr. Bigg W. Both have their thighs broken. At 8.40 PM commenced a trifle bombardment on hostile positions at FOSSE 7 and front & support trenches. Our 100 lachrymatory shell were fired into positions near FOSSE 7	
	7/7/16	-	Quiet day. Nothing to report	
	8/7/16		"Roller Gun" (lone gun of A/77) commenced was cutting. 2" Mort & Shot. Evans R.F.A. was ordered to hospital suffering from appendicitis acute.	
	9/7/16		"Roller Gun" has now cut two gaps in enemy's wire about 25 yards wide & about 10 yards deep. A/77 at 11 PM with 40 May & four 6-horse teams proceeded to HAY ALLEY via LAMBERT'S TRACK. Two limbers were brought with them No 939 which was placed in position at G.14.d.3.0. Our horse was wounded.	

Army Form C. 2118.

WAR DIARY
or
INTELLIGENCE SUMMARY.
(Erase heading not required.)

Instructions regarding War Diaries and Intelligence Summaries are contained in F. S. Regs., Part II. and the Staff Manual respectively. Title pages will be prepared in manuscript.

Place	Date	Hour	Summary of Events and Information	Remarks and references to Appendices
FOSSE 6	10/7/16	-	2nd Lieut A.E. Marson attached T.M. Corner at ST VENANT	
	11/7/16	-	8th R.I.F. made a small raid near HARRISON'S CRATER. C/77 report that the raiding parties were held up & very little information was gained.	
	12/7/16	-	No 31560 Gnr. Fryer, F.A., A"/77 was wounded.	
	13/7/16	-	Hostile Artillery was active between 4 + 5 P.M. shelling our Front + Support Trenches. We retaliated with good effect.	
	14/7/16	-	Orders were received for Lieut. Col. J.H.W. Topp Comd'g 77th Bde. R.F.A., his adjutant, D/77 and a section of B/77 to proceed to ANNIQUIN where they would be attached to 6th Divisional Artillery Group.	
	15/7/16	-	D/77 and the section of B/77 under the command of 2nd Lieut J.E. Edwards took up positions covering 6th Division as follows - D/77, F.30.c.2.4. Section B/77 in CUINCHY RAILWAY STATION. 2nd Lieut W.H. Wadsworth from C/77 was temporarily attached to B/77.	
	16/7/16	-	Major Sir C. Hope-Dunbar, Bart., R.F.A. assumed command of the Brigade from 9 P.M. 15/7/16. D/77 & section of B/77 carried out an extensive bombardment. Capt. C.H. Andrews R.F.A. was appointed Acting Staff Captain 6th Divn. Art'y Group.	
	15/7/16 to 21/7/16		During this period the Bde Comdr. Adjutant, D/77 + section of B/77 were attached to 6th Division. Extensive bombardments have carried out. The main objective of this demonstration was to prevent the removal of any opposing troops down to the SOMME. Both guns of the section of B/77 shortly themselves to pieces and had to be sent to the Workshops on the 19/7/16. In spite of this strenuous work and long hours, the morale of the men was splendid. Telephonic communication went without a hitch.	

Army Form C. 2118.

WAR DIARY
or
INTELLIGENCE SUMMARY.

(Erase heading not required.)

Instructions regarding War Diaries and Intelligence Summaries are contained in F. S. Regs., Part II and the Staff Manual respectively. Title pages will be prepared in manuscript.

Place	Date	Hour	Summary of Events and Information	Remarks and references to Appendices
FOSSE 6	17/7/16	--	Quiet day. Nothing to report	
	18/7/16	--	No 28478 Gnr. Sparks H. was wounded. 2nd Lieut A.E. Mason was evacuated to Hospital	
	19/7/16	}	Nothing to report.	
	20/7/16			
	21/7/16			
	22/7/16		Lt. Colonel J.M.W.Tapp R.F.A. assumed command of the Brigade. D/77 returned to their position at FOSSE 7 and took over the LONE GUN in the CHALK PIT from D/73. D/77 handed over one howitzer to D/70. Section of B/77 took over 2 guns from 8th Divisional Artillery & returned to their position at FOSSE 7	
	23/7/16	--	C/77 moved a section out and relieved A/17 at VERMELLES	
	24/7/16	--	C/77 moved unnecessary section.	
	25/7/16	--	Nothing to report	
	26/7/16	--	D/77 vacated their position at FOSSE 7 and took one position at G.14.c.3/4.3½. 2nd Lt. Wadsworth temporarily attached to B/77 returned to D/77	
	27/7/16	--	Enemy shelled B/77 wagon line causing serious casualties. No.L36155 Gr. Higgs S.L. and No.L37788 Gnr. Bailey J. were killed and No.114133 Gnr. Hayward J., No.L36259 Dr. Bragg T.C., No.L40075 Dr. Cox A.G. wounded. Eight horses had to be destroyed and 3 sent to hospital.	
	28/7/16	--	A raid was carried out by our infantry at 11.40 PM	
	29/7/16		A raid was carried out by hun in trenches during the night 29/30. Raid was unsuccessful. A/77 received a congratulatory message from Royal Anarts Fusiliers on the	

Army Form C. 2118.

WAR DIARY
or
INTELLIGENCE SUMMARY.
(Erase heading not required.)

Instructions regarding War Diaries and Intelligence Summaries are contained in F. S. Regs., Part II and the Staff Manual respectively. Title pages will be prepared in manuscript.

Place	Date	Hour	Summary of Events and Information	Remarks and references to Appendices
FOSSE 6	30/7/16		Quiet day. Nothing to report.	
	31/7/16		Quiet day. During the month hostile shelling has been negligible and most actively on both sides has been with T.Ms. We, however, fired with good effect on trenches and dug outs and kept hostile parties down. Very much less movement has been noticed and it is supposed that men & guns have been withdrawn to meet the offensive down south.	

C. H. Shenkman Capt
for
Lieut Colonel R.F.A.
Comdg 77th Brigade R.F.A.

31/7/16

Army Form C. 2118

WAR DIARY
or
INTELLIGENCE SUMMARY

(Erase heading not required.)

Instructions regarding War Diaries and Intelligence Summaries are contained in F. S. Regs., Part II. and the Staff Manual respectively. Title Pages will be prepared in manuscript.

Place	Date	Hour	Summary of Events and Information	Remarks and references to Appendices
CORONS DE RUTOIRE.	5/7/16	9.0 pm.	A strafe commenced during which 254 rounds were fired. The Hun retaliated with 20 rounds of 5.9's and about 30 lachrymatory shells on Battery position. The strafe lasted until about 10.15 pm.	

Vol 7

WAR DIARY.

77th Brigade RFA

MONTH OF AUGUST, 1916.

VOLUME:— 7

Army Form C. 2118.

WAR DIARY
or
INTELLIGENCE SUMMARY.

(Erase heading not required.)

Sheet I.

Instructions regarding War Diaries and Intelligence Summaries are contained in F. S. Regs., Part II. and the Staff Manual respectively. Title pages will be prepared in manuscript.

Place	Date	Hour	Summary of Events and Information	Remarks and references to Appendices
	1/8/16		Several working parties were dispersed by A/77 also two Trench Mortars were successfully engaged.	
	2/8/16		The day passed very quiet. No artillery activity on the enemy's side.	
	3/8/16		Two rounds were fired in retaliation for enemy shelling on front line by A/77. A hostile aeroplane dropped 3 bombs in the vicinity of Philosophe causing no damage.	
	4/8/16		Several working parties were dispersed by A/77. Trench junction were engaged by A/77. at H19d 35.85, H18d 25.62, H13b 10.05.	
	5/8/16		The day passed very quietly 9 uneventful.	
	6/8/16		There was a little trench mortar activity. A/182 moved into new billets as Mazingarbe.	
	7/8/16		At 12.40 a.m. an S.O.S. Gas Message was received by A/77 which afterwards proved to be false.	
	8/8/16		A/77 retaliated for enemy shelling Dark Street. Batteries registered new zones. There was a gas alarm owing to the enemy putting over smoke in the vicinity of the Hohenzollern.	
	9/8/16		A.A. Uorta at H19d 85.25 was successfully engaged by A/77. On 12.15 A.M. a feint raid was carried out on the front of B/77.	

Army Form C. 2118.

WAR DIARY
or
INTELLIGENCE SUMMARY.

Sheet II

(Erase heading not required.)

Place	Date	Hour	Summary of Events and Information	Remarks and references to Appendices
	9/9/16		An accident occurred at the Wagon Line of B/77 owing to a driver tampering with a fuze. There were four men injured one of who died later.	
	10/9/16		There was considerable trench mortar activity on B/77's front. They retaliated successfully. Several working parties were dispersed with casualties by A/77.	
	11/9/16		Several working parties were dispersed by A/77 & R/77.	
	12/9/16		At 9.45 P.M. B/77 engaged trench mortars at the request of the Infantry. The fire was most effective.	
	13/9/16		Hostile trench mortars were very active & B/77 were continually retaliating. Hostile artillery has increased owing to the fact that Qualch sheet, Zone 7, Leo Porten, Zone 3 & Tenth Avenue was shelled. Several working parties were dispersed by A/77 otherwise the day was uneventful.	
	14/9/16		There was a bombardment of enemy front trenches, support & communication trenches by all batteries.	
	15/9/16		Wire cutting was very effectively carried out at H19 d.4.5 by A/77.	

WAR DIARY
or
INTELLIGENCE SUMMARY.

Army Form C. 2118.

Sheet III.

Place	Date	Hour	Summary of Events and Information	Remarks and references to Appendices
	16/8/16		There was combined hostile trench mortar activity in the LOOS Sector. The day was exceptionally quiet on the other battery fronts.	
	17/8/16		A lot of fresh work was observed on the enemy near trenches. The 9.2" Howr. engaged gun pit at H.32.a.45.90. The shooting was good but no direct hit was obtained on the gun pit. Trenches in the vicinity were considerably damaged.	
	18/8/16		Wire cutting was most successfully carried out at about H.19.d.15.30 by A/77. During the cutting several spots were bombarded.	
	19/8/16		There was considerable trench mortar activity. Several known trench mortar emplacements were engaged by A/77 successfully. The day passed very quietly.	
	20/8/16		Gun was successfully liberated. The enemy put up a heavy barrage.	
	21/8/16		The day passed exceptionally quiet & uneventful.	
	22/8/16		The enemy raided Seaforth crater. Considerable damage was done to our trenches & 30 dud bombs were left behind by the enemy. Our casualties were negligible.	

Army Form C. 2118.

WAR DIARY
or
INTELLIGENCE SUMMARY.

Sheet. IV.

(Erase heading not required.)

Instructions regarding War Diaries and Intelligence Summaries are contained in F. S. Regs., Part II. and the Staff Manual respectively. Title pages will be prepared in manuscript.

Place	Date	Hour	Summary of Events and Information	Remarks and references to Appendices
	23/8/16		Hostile Trench mortars were very active between 6.0 AM to 6.30 AM were silenced by B/77.	
	24/8/16		A/77 & C/77 participated in a feint attack whilst a raid was being carried out by the 8th Bn.	
	25/8/16		The Brigade was reformed on this date as follows:- One section of A/77 joined C/77 etc whole became A/77. One section of A/77 joined B/77 & the whole became B/77. A/162 became C/77 & D/77 remained unchanged. The Brigade proceeded to bivouac by road & remained there until the 29th Aug 1916.	
	29/8/16		The Brigade proceeded to Lillers & entrained for Salenir.	
	30/8/16		The Brigade proceeded by road to Vecquemont prior to going into action.	

C. W. Christie Capt.
for
Lieut Colonel
Comdg 77th Bde R.F.A.

31/8/16

WAR DIARY

77th Brigade R.F.A.

FOR MONTH OF SEPTEMBER, 1916.

VOLUME No 8.

WAR DIARY or INTELLIGENCE SUMMARY

Army Form C. 2118

Place	Date	Hour	Summary of Events and Information	Remarks and references to Appendices
VECQUEMONT	1/9/16		The Brigade in Bivouac en route for the SOMME Front – Preliminary reconnaissances towards MAUREPAS and HARDECOURT.	
	2/9/16		Moved forward to VILLE-SUR-ANCRE and bivouacked. – Rained all night.	
VILLE BRAY	3/9/16		Brigade moved from VILLE to GROVETOWN near BRAY and bivouacked. – Rained all day and night.	
	4/9/16		One section per battery moved up into position at Y WOOD	
MARICOURT MAUREPAS	5/9/16		After moving into action near MAUREPAS STATION "A" and "D" Batteries were heavily shelled, and the following Casualties occurred:— "A" Battery. Killed Bdr. NORTON. Gunners DELLAMORE, COTTON, HUMPHREYS. Wounded 2/Lt. MACKENZIE. Bombardiers ADDIS, TORCOTTE, STUBBS. Gunners HOLMES, BROOKER, FROUDE, WILKEY, WILKINSON, FOLEY, BUTLER, SHOARD. Slightly wounded Capt. GLENDINNING. Shell shock – 2/Lt. RIGBY. Corpl. WALKER. "D" Battery. Capt. ARNOLD. Lt. WISE and Sgt. BOLUS — (wounded by a premature.) Cpl. AVERY. Bdr. THOMAS. Gr. HOWELLS, and Gr. NOLAN the last named subsequently died of wounds. Bdr. MASON of "B" Battery was run over and taken to Hospital. Also Bdr. KINGSTON and Gr. RANDALL of "A" Battery killed. Gr. RANDALL died of wounds. Gr. HUMPHREYS G. of "A" Battery killed. Major F.R. COLLIS wounded. 2/Lt. JOHNSTONE of "D" Battery. The day was spent in Reconnaissance, registration, and digging in, but no material was available for construction of covered cover.	
	7/9/16		Registrations by day; night firing on roads and approaches to COMBLES. Gr. COLLIS of "A" Battery killed. – Lt. JENNER of "C" Battery evacuated to Hospital (sick) Firing all day on barrages as ordered. Our infantry attacked from LEUZE WOOD but failed to reach objective. Heavy German counter attack on LEUZE WOOD partially successful, a portion of the WOOD being recaptured by them.	
	8/9/16		2/Lt. A.G. CHRISTMAS joined from D.A.C. and attached to "C" for M.G.	
	9/9/16		Gunner HOLLAND killed, and a/Bdr. TAYLOR W.H. and Gunner FOSTER & BLYTH wounded – all of "B" Battery. A quiet day generally. 2/Lt. BRISCOE attached to "D" Battery from Bde. HQ. 900 rounds of ammunition – "A" Battery blown up by Shell fire during the night. 2 guns and 72 gunners buried by an 8" Shell, but were all recovered. B.S.M. BROUGH and Cpl. HULL both of B Battery wounded. 2/Lt. DAVIES of D Battery wounded. Driver BALFE, RIMMER, MARSH, & SWADEN wounded at Wagon Line. 4 horses killed and 2 wounded.	
	(7/9/16 10/9/16)		Occasional barrage and night firing on roads. A & B Batteries were shelled and following casualties resulted – Sgt. GLEW. (since died). Bdr. MCHUGH. Gunner COULTER & NOONAN wounded all of "A" Battery. Gunner ROCKALL killed. Sgt. GRAIN. M/Bdr. SMALL. Gunners MASKELL, HATTON, & DIXEY wounded, all of "B" Battery.	
	11/9/16		Brigade Headquarters moved from Y WOOD to MAUREPAS STATION.	

Army Form C. 2118

WAR DIARY
or
INTELLIGENCE SUMMARY
(Erase heading not required.)

Instructions regarding War Diaries and Intelligence Summaries are contained in F.S. Regs., Part II. and Staff Manual respectively. Title Pages will be prepared in manuscript.

Place	Date	Hour	Summary of Events and Information	Remarks and references to Appendices
MAUREPAS	12/9/16		We assisted French attack S. of COMBLES by firing in Barrage. An advance of several hundred yards being made, and a form S.E. of COMBLES taken. The attack was partially successful. The valley was heavily shelled with 5.9 and 8" inches. During the afternoon WALDRON and NORTON turned. These men were dug out and conveyed to hospital. One gun of this battery was put out of action by a direct hit. Gunner HOWARD of A Battery wounded. 2/Lt. RUDDLE joined C Battery.	
	13/9/16		A and D Batteries moved forward to new position beyond ANGLE WOOD. Registrations and night firing on EXITS from COMBLES, MORVAL and BOULEAUX WOOD.	
	14/9/16		Infant Dug-outs and Gun Platforms. 2/Lts. HAGARTY, COBBOLD and HEATH joined and were posted to B, C, and D Batteries respectively.	
	15/9/16		Firing in Barrage, and registering as ordered. Gunners MAYER and HAGAR wounded – both in A Battery. Barrage was maintained on COMBLES TRENCH all day. L. attacking our infantry gained their first objective. Last Division on left failed to get BOULEAUX WOOD, and the advance towards MORVAL and LES BOEUFS did not get through.	
	16/9/16		Kept up Barrage as ordered.	
	17/9/16		Engaged and silenced enemys battery in T 17 – otherwise a quiet day.	
	18/9/16		Barrage as ordered. Light too bad all day for observation, again engaged battery in T 17 C.	
	19/9/16		A quiet day.	
	20/9/16		Huns were dispersed at T.21.d.7½. O. by B battery. The day was spent in registration of the MORVAL zone. One gun in D Battery out of action owing to broken buffer springs.	
	21/9/16		Registrations continued. Major A.E. NEWLANDS of C Battery evacuated to Hospital (sick). 2/Lt. O.S. BURKE carried on in his absence.	
	22/9/16		A quiet day. Registration of MORVAL conducted. Night firing on roads and exits from MORVAL.	
	23/9/16		A quiet day. Night firing on COMBLES and exits.	
	24/9/16		Barrage kept up as ordered, also registrations, and night firing on trenches from BOULEAUX WOOD to MORVAL, exits from MORVAL and COMBLES and trench in T 12 C. Cpl. MORTON of A battery, and Bdr. TURNER of B battery wounded. Gun disabled on 20/9/16 returned to D battery from J.O.M.	
	25/9/16		We took part in the attack on MORVAL, keeping up Barrage in support of 56th Divl. Infantry as ordered. The attack on MORVAL, BOULEAUX WOOD and LES BOEUF was successful, and all objectives were attained by 6 p.m. Enemy many tried from MORVAL defences down to the COMBLES VALLEY; also many parties of Germans were caught on the S.E. of MORVAL and dispersed. Many were seen walking out of MORVAL with their hands above their heads.	

1875 Wt. W593/826 1,000,000 4/15 J.B.C. & A. A.D.S.S./Forms/C.2118.

WAR DIARY
INTELLIGENCE SUMMARY
(Erase heading not required.)

Army Form C. 2118

Place	Date	Hour	Summary of Events and Information	Remarks and references to Appendices
MAUREPAS	25/9/16		2/Lt. O.S. BURKE while doing duty as F.O.O. was killed by a bullet from an enemy sniper. Gunner HUTTRIDGE of B battery was slightly wounded, but retained his duty.	
ANGLE WOOD	26/9/16		COMBLES having fallen, advanced positions were reconnoitred in the COMBLES RAVINE.	
COMBLES	27/9/16		Major COLLIS and 2/Lt. R.G. HAMILTON R.F.A., D. Battery was killed by shell fire while reconnoitring for forward gun positions. Capt. R. HOPKINS R.A.M.C. was wounded by the same shell, and died shortly afterwards. In the evening Batteries came out of action, and guns were removed to the wagon lines, where they remained till the end of the month.	
	28/9/16		Ammunition was removed from Gun Line to Wagon Lines near CARNOY. The three Officers killed on 27/9/16 were buried in CARNOY Cemetery.	
	29/9/16		Surplus Ammunition was returned to the D.A.C. Capt. M.E. MOIR joined D battery and took over command. A quiet day.	
	30/9/16		The withdrawal of the Batteries from the Gun Line was carried out satisfactorily and without casualties. The amount of sickness during the month was well below average. The men worked well and cheerfully under the most adverse circumstances, both in regard that matter conditions and also at times under heavy shell fire. Communications with Batteries and Infantry Headquarters were, on the whole, well maintained, notwithstanding considerable damage to the lines caused by shell fire and traffic. The morale of the men during this trying month was excellent, and the commendatory letter of General Hickie referring to the shooting of the 16th Divl. Artillery on the Somme front as "glorious" while greatly appreciated by the Brigade, was felt to be not unmerited.	

10/10/16

J.W. Tapp
Lt. Col.
Cmdg. 77th Bde., R.F.A.

WAR DIARY

MONTH OF OCTOBER, 1916.

VOLUME 9

77th Brigade R.F.A.

Army Form C. 2118.

77th Brigade, R.F.A. WAR DIARY or INTELLIGENCE SUMMARY.

(Erase heading not required.)

Instructions regarding War Diaries and Intelligence Summaries are contained in F.S. Regs., Part II. and the Staff Manual respectively. Title pages will be prepared in manuscript.

Place	Date	Hour	Summary of Events and Information	Remarks and references to Appendices
CARNOY	1/10/16	4.30 a.m.	The Brigade having been at the Wagon Line since the evening of the 24th September (date of coming out of action at the SOMME) marched to TALMAS in fine weather, and went into billets for the night	
TALMAS	2/10/16		Left TALMAS and marched to AMPLIER – a very wet day; billeted	
AMPLIER	3/10/16		Left AMPLIER and marched to VACQUERIE-LE-BOUCQ and again went into billets. Heavy rainstorms were experienced on the march.	
VACQUERIE				
HEUCHIN	4/10/16		Left VACQUERIE and moved on to HEUCHIN – another wet day	
QUIESTEDE	5/10/16		Marched from HEUCHIN to QUIESTEDE	
GODEWEARSVELDE	6/10/16 7/10/16 8/10/16		From QUIESTEDE to GODEWEARSVELDE where the Brigade went into billets until the 9th October. The Brigade rested at GODEWEARSVELDE while the Brigade Commander and Battery Commanders went forward to reconnoitre the new positions about to be taken over. During the 6 days march from the SOMME extremely wet weather was experienced. In the greater part of the time, and the roads for the most part were very heavy. Supplies were obtained from various refilling points en-route, and the troops were provided with a hot meal every day. The average time of moving off was 6 a.m. Reveille being from 2 to 3 hours earlier. Several men fell out exhausted on the 5th and an ambulance had to be fetched from AIRE. One horse (in D battery) dropped dead in the Lines on the 6th Oct. Apart from these there were no casualties.	
WESTOUTRE	9/10/16		The Brigade marched to WESTOUTRE where A, B and C batteries halted at wagon lines, D battery moving on to their wagon line at MONT NOIR.	
	10/10/16		Two sections of A/77 came into position at N.15.c.2.7. and one section of D/77 at N.14.c.9.8. Another section of B and the remaining section of D moved up into position, and the whole was completed only 4 guns of B/18 Fd. batteries being in action. The whole of C Battery remained at the Wagon Line at WESTOUTRE from the 9th to the 16th Oct., where much was carried on at the horse-standings, shelters, making roads & motor troughs, and general improvements in preparation for winter.	
	11/10/16 12/10/16 13/10/16 14/10/16 15/10/16 16/10/16		Registering targets. Checking Lines and Connector. Registration difficult owing to high wind. Further Registration. Retaliated for active trench mortar fire on our front line trenches. Registration including night lines. Further registration; checking night lines and retaliating for T.M. fire on front line trenches. Registrating T.M. emplacements, night lines checked. Night lines. A.D.S.S./form/C.2118. Magumi retaliated for T.M. fire on front line. 2/Lt. R. Randle evacuated to Hospital (Sick)	

2353. Wt. W23141454 700,000 5/15 D.D.&L.

77th Brigade, R.F.A.
Army Form C. 2118.

WAR DIARY or INTELLIGENCE SUMMARY

(Erase heading not required.)

Instructions regarding War Diaries and Intelligence Summaries are contained in F.S. Regs., Part II. and the Staff Manual respectively. Title pages will be prepared in manuscript.

Place	Date	Hour	Summary of Events and Information	Remarks and references to Appendices
WESTOUTRE	16/10/16		S.O.S. test. A quiet day. C Battery became attached for tactical purposes to the "Left group", and took over the position occupied by D/180 at N.10.a.½.7½, and the relief was completed on the evening of the 19th Oct. Guns were taken over with the position, D/180 taking over the guns of 9/77 at the wagon line. The personnel of 9/77 with exception of the B.C., section Commanders & detachments remained at the wagon line. Major Sir Charles Stape-Dunbar took command of the new Left group. Capt. the Hon. J.L. Nugent taking command of B battery. On the night 17/18, and again on the night 18/19, three guns pits of C. battery were seriously flooded, and on the 19th Oct. by order of Lt-Col group a new position was were taken up at N.10.C.8.O. 2/Lt. H.O. Leal evacuated to hospital (sick).	
	17/10/16			
	18/10/16 19/10/16 20/10/16		Quiet days, nothing to record. No. 43704 Driver Walker W.W. was awarded the military medal, & parchment certificate for gallantry in the field, in that he while at LOOS on April 27th and 29th, and again on Sept. 15th at OAKHANGER WOOD, repeatedly went out to repair telephone wires under very heavy fire, with disregard to personal safety.	
	21/10/16 22/10/16		A quiet day. No. 19979 Sgt. G. Henry and 70782 Gunner Willoford H. who were recommended for conspicuous gallantry at the SOMME were handed parchment certificates by the Brigade Commander.	
	23/24/10/16		Quiet days - more registrations were carried out, and retaliation for T.M. fire. Registered targets by balloon.	
	27/10/16 28/10/16 29/10/16		More registration — retaliated for T.M. fire. Retaliated for T.M. and M.G. Gun fire. and assisted aeroplane movements. Find barrage on first line trenches and communication trenches, and assisted in a successful raid on MAEDELSTEDE FARM. The raid was carried out by the 49th Infantry Brigade, and was successful & prisoners being taken, + dug outs destroyed. Infantry reported that hostile fire was accurate and effective. 2/Lt J.A. Huddleson joined and was posted to A/77.	
	30/10/16 31/10/16		Retaliated for heavy T.M. fire, and 77 m.m. fire. Heavy enemy shelling takes place by day and night, but enemy's first days and, has hampered the movement of troops in gun position and transport lines. That & check with D.D.& L.T [ADSS North Corps] have been made in preparation for the winter 2/Lt H.O. Leal and X.Y. Mickelson joined and one posted to B/77 and 9/77 respectively.	

(17/10/16)

WAR DIARY.

FOR

MONTH OF NOVEMBER, 1916.

VOLUME 10.

114th Brigade A.F.A.

Army Form C. 2118.

WAR DIARY
or
INTELLIGENCE SUMMARY.
(Erase heading not required.)

77th Brigade R.F.A. for Month of November 1916

Instructions regarding War Diaries and Intelligence Summaries are contained in F.S. Regs., Part II. and Staff Manual respectively. Title pages will be prepared in manuscript.

Place	Date 1916	Hour	Summary of Events and Information	Remarks and references to Appendices
FERMOY FARM N.13.d.2.0 (near LOCRE)	Nov. 1st	-	2nd Lieut. K.G. WILLIAMS, Comdg "C"/77 wounded in action and evacuated to hospital. 2nd Lieut. L.W. HEATH trans. furd from D/77 to take command of C/77 vice 2Lt. Williams. Quiet day. Lieut. Colonel J.H.W. Tapp comdg 77th Bde. R.F.A. evacuated to hospital sick. Major Surg. E.D. HOPE D.S.O. B.S.A. assumed command of the Brigade vice Lt. Col. Tapp to hospital. Enemy trench mortars fairly active during the day. Howitzer hostility to report.	
	3rd	-	Quiet day	
	4th	-	2nd Lieut. R.W. BRISCOE evacuated to hospital, sick. Occasional Rifle Grens, aerial on enemy front & support line. Enemy retaliated on our front line and Van Keep.	
	5th	-	Enemy trench mortars active – our retaliation effective.	
	6th	-	Quiet day. Enemy trenches near PETIT BOIS appear badly damaged since bombardment on 4th Nov.	
	7th	-	Rows dug 97th. Infantry Brigade was unsuccessful.	
	8th	-	Slight Enemy trench mortar activity	
	9th	-	Quiet day - nothing to report	
	10th	-	Enemy barrage now active than usual - nothing to report	
	11th	-	Slight Enemy Trench mortar activity - own 4.5" effectively dealt with them	
	12th	-	Enemy trench mortars very active. Enemy "Kitty" (heavy T.M.) fired the past own air aircraft very high up here in the line of flight from a lighter T.M. is also "KITTY" was effectively dealt with. To confuse our observers "KITTY" was effectively dealt with.	

Army Form C. 2118.

WAR DIARY
or
INTELLIGENCE SUMMARY.
(Erase heading not required.)

77th Brigade R.F.A. for month of November 1916

Place	Date 1916	Hour	Summary of Events and Information	Remarks and references to Appendices
FERMOY FARM	Nov. 13.	-	Quiet day.	
	14.	-	Quiet day.	
	15.			
	16.			
	17.	-	Enemy artillery more active than usual	
	18.	-	Observation difficult. Enemy 4.2" How appeared to be making intensive registration	
	19.	-	Enemy T.M's (EVE & RUTH) were active. Our retaliation soon silenced them.	
	20.	-	Slight enemy T.M activity	
	21.			
	22.			
	23.			
	24.	-	Quiet days	
	25.			
	26.			
	27.	-	Enemy T.M activity was effectively dealt with. Our activity above normal.	
	28.	-	Foggy days - Observation impossible. Quiet days.	
	29.			
	30.			

C.S. Hope Dunbar
Major R.F.A.
Comdg 77th Bde R.F.A.

WAR DIARY FOR MONTH OF DECEMBER, 1916.

VOLUME 11

77 Brigade R.F.A.

WAR DIARY or INTELLIGENCE SUMMARY

Army Form C. 2118.

Place	Date 1916	Hour	Summary of Events and Information	Remarks and references to Appendices
FERMOY FARM. N18.d.2.0. (Near LOCRE)	DEC 1st		Quiet day.	
	2nd		Enemy T.M.'s and Artillery fired on our front line and support trenches in retaliation for our Stokes Guns bombardment midday.	
	3rd		Enemy Artillery active. Apparently registering. Bad light all day.	
	4th		Fairly quiet day. Enemy shelled our working parties at railroad. 2/Lt R.W. BRISCOE evacuated to England.	
	5th		Light quiet day. Enemy Artillery active. No movement seen and no aeroplane activity. 2/Lt A.E. GOATMAN, 2/Lt W.D. FEATHERSTONE & 2/Lt J.C.B. HUNT joined. Posted 2/Lt to C/77.	
	6th		Enemy shelled support line and communication trenches. Light had all day. On the whole fairly quiet.	18 C/77
	7th		Quiet day. Haywire, and observation impossible. 2/Lt P.H.B. FITCH joined Bde & posted to D/77.	
	8th		Quiet day. Haywire.	
	9th		Quiet day. Light rain during first part of the day.	
	10th		Quiet day. Observation fair. 2/Lt F.L.L. DAVIES joined Bde & posted to D/77.	
	11th		Very quiet day. Observation fair. A large explosion occurred at about N16.c or N16.a. Probably a heavy T.M. A large detonation caused it at 11pm but there was no smoke and N.T.M. was observed to burst. Capt. H.G. GLENDINNING evacuated to England.	
	12th		Very quiet day. Observation impossible owing to snow, sleet and mist.	
	13th		Fairly good observation. Working parties were spotted in trench at N24 & 35.40. Enemy Artillery and T.M.'s active	
	14th		Quiet day.	
	15th		Observation fair. Weather continues impossible for observation.	
	16th		Quiet day. HARNAH's suggested and allowed at 2.50 P.M.	
	17th		Very quiet day. Very misty and unfavourable for observation.	
	18th		A large phosphorus bomb thrown bunk at 7.15 pm. Just seeing 108° from N16.d.45.25 HAZEL egged and burst at 3.55P - 2/Lt A.G. CHRISTMAS evacuated to England.	
	19th		Very quiet day. Enemy Artillery active during morning. Working parties spotted and dispersed at Q.19 & 60.80 & near T.am.o.	
	20th		Observation very fair. Enemy A/dingpots.	
	21st		Very quiet day. Light misty.	
	22nd		Observation poor.	
	23rd		Excellent light. Very early day. Enemy Artillery and Aircraft very active. HARNAH active in af Kencos.	
	24th		Xmas day. Enemy Artillery active at 10 am.	
	25th		Good observation.	
	26th		Very quiet day. Enemy A/Alling active during the morning.	
	27th		Observation poor. No aeroplanes in action during the day, Mostly working parties were at N18 & 42.10.	
	28th		Very quiet day.	
	29th		Maj Sir C.WADE JONES R.H.A. joined the Battery. Lt Col T.M. ARCYDALE, R.S.O. resumed command of the Bde.	
	30th		Observation fair. Enemy A/tilling active.	
	31st			

T.M. Archdale.
Lt Col D.S.O. R.H.A.
Cmdg. 77th Bde R.F.A.

www.ingramcontent.com/pod-product-compliance
Lightning Source LLC
Chambersburg PA
CBHW081443160426
43193CB00013B/2364